T4-AVB-122

SYSTEM
44
TM

Teaching Resources
for the *System 44* Library

Upper Elementary

All rights reserved   Published by Scholastic Inc.   Printed in the U.S.A.

ISBN-13: 978-0-439-74173-6
ISBN-10: 0-439-74173-4

SCHOLASTIC, SYSTEM 44, SCHOLASTIC READING COUNTS!, SCHOLASTIC READING INVENTORY, READ 180, and associated logos and designs are trademarks and/or registered trademarks of Scholastic Inc. LEXILE and LEXILE FRAMEWORK are registered trademarks of MetaMetrics, Inc. Other company names, brand names, and product names are the property and/or trademarks of their respective owners.

1 2 3 4 5 6 7 8 9 10   10   17 16 15 14 13 12 11 10 09 08

Table of Contents

Conference Guides and Wrap-Ups

Additional Resources

Introduction to the *System 44* Library

The *System 44* Library is a collection of 36 high-interest, age-appropriate texts for struggling readers. The Library provides opportunities for students who are developing decoding skills to apply their skills to motivating, relevant texts that use the language and features of authentic fiction and nonfiction texts. The books promote practice and review of essential phonics concepts in text that is controlled for difficulty. The purpose of the *System 44* Library is to:

- engage students with high-interest, age-appropriate fiction and nonfiction texts that promote successful independent reading practice and reading enjoyment.

- practice phonics skills and build on students' expanding knowledge of sound-spelling correspondences and high-frequency words.

- build fluency through independent practice, repeated reading, and teacher instruction.

- build vocabulary through repeated exposure to content-specific and general academic vocabulary words.

- build endurance with increasingly longer and more challenging text.

- develop listening comprehension through use of audiobooks.

Library Components

System 44 Library

The 36 books in the *System 44* Library cover diverse genres and topics. These books have been analyzed using the Lexile Framework®—a highly accurate system that matches students to materials at their level so they can read with success.

These books provide opportunities for students to review and practice decoding and fluency skills introduced on the *System 44* Software and in the *Teaching Guide.* Important phonics and word study elements—called Phonics Focus—are listed on the inside back cover of each book and on the Library Overview on **pages 10–15** of this guide.

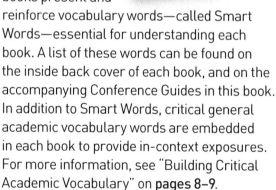

Additionally, the books present and reinforce vocabulary words—called Smart Words—essential for understanding each book. A list of these words can be found on the inside back cover of each book, and on the accompanying Conference Guides in this book. In addition to Smart Words, critical general academic vocabulary words are embedded in each book to provide in-context exposures. For more information, see "Building Critical Academic Vocabulary" on **pages 8–9**.

The *System 44* Library books gradually increase in difficulty, as shown in the chart below.

	Books 1–16	Books 17–28	Books 29–36
Software Connection	Series 1–10	Series 11–18	Series 19–25
Lexile®	100–250	200–350	300–450
Page Count	8–16 pp.	16–24 pp.	24–32 pp.
Smart Words	3–5	6	7
Art	Art on every page	Art on approximately every 3 pages	Art on approximately every 4 pages

Teaching Resources for the *System 44* Library

This book is organized into the following sections:

- **Using the *System 44* Library in the Classroom** This section provides instructions for using the Conference Guides, Wrap-Ups, and Routines in the classroom.

- **red.** **Building Critical Academic Vocabulary** This article presents background and practical information for developing academic vocabulary through independent reading.

- **Library Overview** This chart provides at-a-glance information regarding Library titles, genres, Phonics Focus, Smart Words (including Spanish cognates), and general academic vocabulary words.

- **red.** **Routines** Teaching routines may be used with the Conference Guides to help reinforce decoding skills, vocabulary-building strategies, and fluency skills.

- **Conference Guides** Teaching resources for each Library title present book summaries and resources for conferencing and reinforcing decoding, vocabulary, fluency, and comprehension skills.

- **Wrap-Ups** These reproducible practice pages, also available through the Scholastic Achievement Manager (SAM), provide students with comprehension and writing activities to promote accountable reading.

- **Graphic Organizers** The reproducible Word Sort, Vocabulary Builder, and Fluency Checklist provide additional support for building decoding skills, vocabulary, and fluency.

- **Reading Log** This reproducible graphic organizer allows students to track their reading progress.

- **Answer Key** Answers are provided for the activities in the Wrap-Up pages.

System 44 Audiobooks

Recordings of each book may be used to scaffold student access to the text, and to promote listening comprehension. The audiobooks present two voices:

- **The Reading Coach,** who introduces the book, previews the book's Smart Words and Phonics Focus, and prompts students to react to the story.

- **The Narrator,** who reads aloud, modeling fluent reading of the text.

System 44 Reading Counts! Quizzes

Scholastic Reading Counts! quizzes provide computer-based multiple-choice questions for each *System 44* Library book. These quizzes help you monitor successful book completion. (See the *Assessment and Reporting Guide* for additional information.)

Using the *System 44* Library in the Classroom

The phonic elements targeted in the *System 44* Library are based on a scope and sequence that gradually increases in difficulty. You may wish to have students read the books in order, assign books based on Lexile (use SAM reports to access students' Lexile scores), or have students choose books based on their own preferences. The following is recommended procedure for using these books:

1 **Preview** Begin by previewing the book. Read the title and back cover information. Point out the Phonics Focus words and Smart Words listed on the inside back cover. Tell students that the Phonics Focus words present examples of sounds, patterns, or word parts they will encounter often as they read the book. Explain that the Smart Words are vocabulary words they will encounter as they read the book. Preview Smart Word definitions (given at the beginning of the book) with students, or have students listen to the audiobook to hear a recorded introduction to the Smart Words.

2 **Discuss and Monitor** Have students read the book independently, with a partner, or with your support as needed. Recordings of each book may be used to scaffold student access to the text and build listening comprehension. During and after reading, use the book summary and comprehension questions in the Conference Guide to engage students in discussion and to monitor comprehension. To foster accountable reading and provide comprehension and writing practice, have students complete the Wrap-Up activity provided for each book.

3 **Instruct** Use the resources provided in the Conference Guides to assess students' need for instruction in decoding, vocabulary building, and fluency related to their reading. Follow the directions in the Conference box for each instructional option. In cases where there is a need for further instruction, proceed to the Individualized Instruction box.

4 **Reinforce** Use the Routines provided on **pages 16–29** in this book to remediate and reinforce skills.

5 **Record** Guide students to use the Vocabulary Builder on **page 103**, Fluency Checklist on **page 104**, and Reading Log on **page 105** to record their progress.

6 **Assess and Track Progress** Use *Scholastic Reading Counts!* electronic quizzes to assess book completion and generate progress reports.

System 44 Library Conference Guides

Conference with students to build skills, promote accountability, and guide reading response.

Phonics Focus
Indicates the Phonics Focus of the book.

Book Summary
Gives a brief book synopsis for teacher reference.

Wrap-Up
Provides student materials for comprehension and writing practice that may be photocopied or printed from SAM and distributed to students.

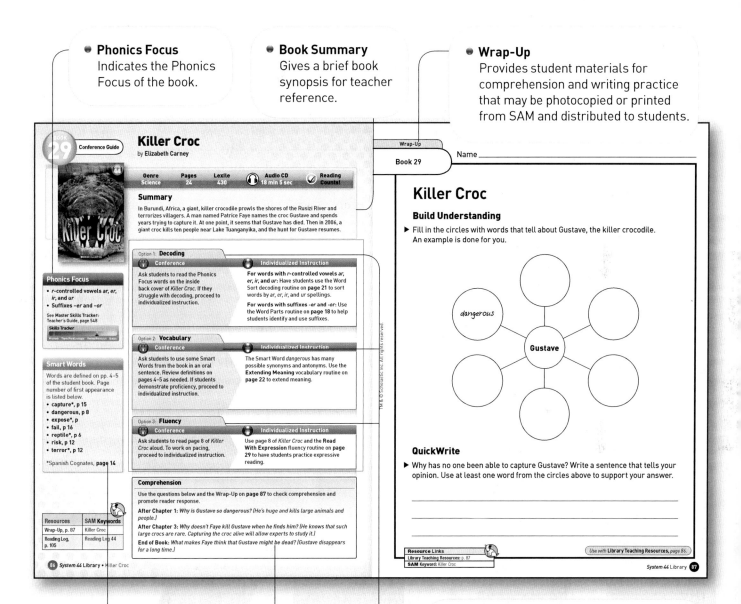

Smart Words
Lists the Smart Words that are highlighted and explained in the book.

Comprehension Questions
Offers engaging questions to promote oral discussion of the book and monitor comprehension.

Instructional Options
Provides a plan for quickly surveying students' grasp of decoding skills and vocabulary associated with the book, as well as their reading fluency. For each instructional option, assess the need for instruction by following the directions in the Conference box. Progress to Individualized Instruction as needed.

Vocabulary Development

- The average student learns 2,000 to 3,000 words each year, mostly by reading words in context.
- Instruction for struggling readers should help students learn morphologically connected academic words through repeated in-context encounters.

Students need frequent opportunities for independent reading of texts that contain critical general academic words in context.

Dr. Elfrieda H. Hiebert

Building Critical Academic Vocabulary

What Is Academic Vocabulary?

In the middle grades, students are faced with textbooks that present a vast increase in the amount and complexity of academic vocabulary. This is when students with vocabulary problems begin to struggle (RAND Reading Study Group, 2002).

There are different types of academic vocabulary. One type, technical vocabulary, includes subject-specific words. Usually these words are introduced to students as the focus of content-area instruction (Graves, 2000), so that students will learn terms like *democracy* and *oligarchy* in the social studies classroom and terms like *photosynthesis* and *cytoplasm* in the science classroom as these concepts are being introduced.

Another category of academic vocabulary, sub-technical or general academic vocabulary (Coxhead, 2000), consists of more general words such as *consider*, *system*, *form*, and *structure* that appear across multiple subjects. General academic words vary in meaning in different contexts and act as different parts of speech. For example, a science text may describe the *form* that matter takes, while a social studies text may describe the way in which a government was *formed* .

While general academic words are just as crucial to academic success as technical vocabulary, they are not often deliberately taught. In addition, since they appear infrequently in non-academic texts, students are less likely to learn these words outside of the classroom.

The Critical Academic Word List (CAWL)

Many of the general academic vocabulary words incorporated throughout the *System 44* Library come from the Critical Academic Word List (Hiebert, 2008). Unlike other lists of general academic words that were developed for university students learning English as a second language (Coxhead, 2000), the Critical Academic Word List (CAWL) was specifically designed to include the general academic words most critical to the academic success of elementary- and middle-school students.

Determining Which Words Make the List

To compile the CAWL, researchers used the following criteria:

1. **Frequency** The list contains words predicted to appear with at least moderate frequency in elementary- and middle-grade texts, particularly content-area texts.

2 **Morphological Richness** According to Carlisle and Katz (2006), words that appear with some frequency increase the likelihood of recognition of other members of their morphological family. While the word *visualize* is rare, *visual, vision, visible,* and *invisible* occur with moderate frequency in written texts. The CAWL, therefore, includes less commonly occurring words that are part of semantically linked morphological families. This inclusion enables teachers to direct students' attention to similarities and differences between the meanings of words within each family.

3 **Dispersion** This term refers to the degree to which words appear across different subject areas. A word such as *form* appears across many subject areas, while a word such as *adverb* appears mostly in the context of language arts. The CAWL contains words dispersed widely across different subject areas.

The CAWL in Practice: Word Learning Strategies

Research indicates that the average student learns from 2,000 to 3,000 words each year, and that most of this learning is done by reading words in context, not through approaches that attempt to teach words one at a time (Anderson & Nagy, 1992).

Students need frequent opportunities for independent reading of texts that contain critical words in context. The books in the *System 44* Library provide students with repeated exposures to words from the CAWL. Each book contains a list of Smart Words that includes selected general academic vocabulary words from the CAWL as well as content-specific vocabulary words that are essential for book comprehension. Additionally, scaffolded vocabulary support is presented at the back of each book and in this guide.

Differentiating Instruction

✓ **Reinforcing Book Vocabulary** Guide students to review the Smart Words and their definitions provided in each book, and use the audiobooks to build meta-cognitive awareness of these words. Discuss word meaning and have students use words in sentences.

✓ **Morphological Word Families** Foster students' word consciousness by associating Smart Words with related words. Use the Extending Meaning vocabulary routine on **page 22** to guide students to make connections among words.

✓ **Vocabulary Building Practice** Teach strategies to help students unlock word meaning through word analysis and context clues. See the Multiple-Meaning Words Routine on **page 23** and the Context Clues Routine on **page 24**.

✓ **Independent Application** Encourage students to use the Vocabulary Builder graphic organizer on **page 103** to record and learn new words they encounter during reading.

References

• Anderson, R., and Nagy, W. (1992). "The Vocabulary Conundrum." *American Educator* (16)4, 14–18.

• Carlisle, J.F. & Katz, L. A. (2006). "Effects of Word and Morpheme Familiarity on Reading of Derived Words." *Reading and Writing, 19,* 669–693.

• Coxhead, A. (2000). "A New Academic Word List." *TESOL Quarterly,* 34(2), 213–238.

• Graves, M. F. (2000). "A Vocabulary Program to Complement and Bolster a Middle-Grade Comprehension Program." In B. M. Taylor, M. F. Graves, & P. van Den Broek.

• Hiebert E.H. (2008). "Identifying a Critical Form of Vocabulary in Middle-Grade, Content-Area Texts." [Online] Available: http://www.textproject.org

• RAND Reading Study Group (2000). "Reading for Understanding: Toward a Research and Development Program in Reading Comprehension." Washington, DC: RAND.

Library Overview Lexile range 100–250

This chart provides an overview of the Lexile, genre, Phonics Focus, and vocabulary coverage of each book. Vocabulary coverage includes:

- **Smart Words:** Words essential for understanding each book that students should attend to before, during, and after reading.

- **General Academic Words:** Critical general academic words embedded in each book to provide in-context exposures. For more information on general academic words, see "Building Critical Academic Vocabulary" on **pages 8–9.**

Title	Genre	Phonics Focus	Smart Words (With Spanish Cognates)	General Academic Words
1. **Hunt & Kill: A Look at Predators** LEXILE 240	science	✔ **Short vowels** (big, cat, dig, egg, fed, get, it, log, mad, mud, nab, rip, sit, top, up) ✔ **Consonants** *b,d, g,* and *p* (bad, big, dig, but, egg, fed, get, log, mad, mud, nab, rip, top)	attack *(atacar)* predator *(depredador)* prey	attack, attacks, need, person
2. **Messy Jobs** LEXILE 150	jobs	✔ **Short vowels** (bags, big, bin, bits, can, cuts, dig, fixes, fun, gets, has, hits, in, is, it, job, lots, man, mixes, rocks, rots, wins) ✔ **–s and –es endings** (bits, cuts, digs, dips, fixes, gets, lots, mixes, rocks, rots, wins)	machine *(máquina)* stink waste	machine
3. **Sports Bloopers** LEXILE 200	social studies	✔ **s blends** (scab, skill, skip, slam, slip, snaps, sped, spell, spot, stands, step, stop) ✔ **Double consonants** (huff, puff, stuff, fell, skill, spell, grass, mess, miss, pass)	bounce score skill	skill
4. **Fast! The World's Fastest Couch and Other Fast Things** LEXILE 150	science	✔ **Blends** (blast, brisk, desk, fast, glad, grip, must, plan, plant, rest, risk, sprigs, strap, trip, twigs, twins)	limit *(límite)* rate vehicle *(vehículo)*	rate, reach, travel
5. **I Do Not Eat Worms (and Other Poems)** LEXILE 140	poetry	✔ **Review blends** (class, dress, skill, smells, spell, spill, still, stuff) ✔ **-ng and -nk** (sing, sink) ✔ **Double consonants** (smells, spell, spill, still, stuff)	express *(expresar)* journal poem *(poema)*	express
6. **Wonders of the World** LEXILE 240	social studies	✔ **Blends** (act, gift, help, lift, plants, ramp, send, sent, stand, went)	build statue *(estatua)* wonder	act, attacks, moved, united
7. **Mystery Photo** LEXILE 240	science	✔ **Closed syllables** (baskets, biggest, contest, hidden, invent, linen, napkin, objects, panic, sunset, traffic)	guess hint invent *(inventar)* mystery *(misterio)* ordinary *(ordinario— can also mean "vulgar" or "common")*	construct, invented, mystery, need, objects, power, solve, usually

Title	Genre	Phonics Focus	Smart Words (With Spanish Cognates)	General Academic Words
8 **Travels With Mapman** LEXILE 240	social studies	✔ *sh* (crash, dash, finish, fish, gash, gushes, mash, rush, shift, ships, shut, splash, wishes)	**border** **capital** *(capital)* **coast** *(costa)* **island** *(isla)* **ocean** *(océano)*	body, border, circle, compete, locate, national, need, simple, travel, united
9 **The Gift** LEXILE 250	classic retelling	✔ *ch, -tch* (bunch, check, Chet, ditch, hunch, lunch, match, much, rich, switch)	**buy** **choose** **cost** *(costar)* **receive** *(recibir)* **special** *(especial)*	special
10 **Gross Bugs!** LEXILE 190	science	✔ *th* (path, thanks, that, them, then, thin, think, this, with)	**active** *(activo/a)* **destroy** *(destruir)* **itch** **outdoors** **type** *(tipo)*	body, damage, destroy, group, follow, move, travel, type, types
11 **Signs** LEXILE 200	social studies	✔ *-ing* ending with no base change (bending, ending, happening, helping, shocking, telling) ✔ Review of *ch, -tch, sh, th* (batch, catch, check, match, shocking, Spanish, that, them, think, this)	**allow** **drive** **sign** **traffic** *(tráfico)* **warn**	allowed, circle, danger, matter, mean, means, sign, signs, traveling, warn
12 **Fashion Flashback** LEXILE 220	social studies	✔ *-ed* ending with no base change (acted, blasted, dressed, ended, expected, fixed, instructed, jazzed, lasted, lifted, limited, matched, missed, packed, shifted, shocked, stacked, stomped, tricked, wished)	**decade** *(década)* **fashion** **popular** *(popular)* **practical** *(práctico/a)* **trend**	fashion, history, introduction, popular, rule, simple, trend
13 **Button Your Lip and Other Idioms** LEXILE 210	language arts	✔ Closed syllables with schwa (button, common, finish, gossip, happens, jacket, kitchen, kitten, piglets, problem)	**common** *(común)* **explain** *(explicar)* **idiom** **shake** **tale**	explain, explains, mean, means, need, person, true
14 **African Journey** LEXILE 230	science	✔ Consonants + *-al, -el,* or *-le* (animals, cattle, jungle, little, mammals, middle, rental, simple, single, travel)	**local** *(local)* **migrate** *(migrar)* **national** *(nacional)* **nature** *(naturaleza)* **travel**	attack, circle, energy, group, guide, labeled, national, photo, raise, travel
15 **Ripped From the Headlines** LEXILE 210	social studies	✔ Long *a* with final *e* (blaze, brave, came, grade, grave, lane, made, plane, plate, safe, save, tales, waves) ✔ Long *i* with final *e* (crime, fine, fire, five, hike, inside, life, pipe, ride, side, time, wide)	**amaze** **believe** **brave** **danger** **rescue** *(rescatar)*	act, acted, aid, amaze, amazed, choice, energy, formed, move, normal, protect, survive, true
16 **Win or Lose?** LEXILE 210	fiction	✔ Soft *c* and *g* (ace, chance, face, gentle, Grace, judge, nice, nudge, place, raged, ranged, twice) ✔ Suffixes *-ment* and *-ness* (equipment, statement, sadness)	**coach** **important** *(importante)* **kick** **practice** *(práctica)* **team**	agreement, amazement, equipment, excited, family, gentle, grace, important, mean, moved, practice, range, rules, sign

Library Overview Lexile range 200–350

Title	Genre	Phonics Focus	Smart Words (With Spanish Cognates)	General Academic Words
(17) **Cool Jobs in Basketball** LEXILE 300	jobs	✔ Words with VCe (advice, athlete, came, collide, combine, compete, desires, dispute, drove, games, grades, hired, hires, hope, huge, inside, Jones, made, name, notes, promote, relate, shape, site, spoke, whole, woke, write) ✔ Prefixes non- and un- (nonathletes, nonstop, unexpected, unpacks)	athlete *(atleta)* business experience *(experiencia)* hire intern *(interno/a)* rely	able, advice, appear, base, became, combine, combined, confides, decisions, desires, encouraged, exercises, experience, realized, relate, special
(18) **Meet the Dragon Slayers** LEXILE 330	social studies	✔ Ending -ing (killing, shocking) ✔ Ending -ing with base change (running, saving, zipping)	accident *(accidente)* crew emergency *(emergencia)* respond *(responder)* training *(entrenamiento)* volunteer *(voluntario/a)*	charged, chief, dangerous, depend, means, need, needed, person, prepared, respond, serve, survive
(19) **Crash!** LEXILE 320	science	✔ -ed with no base change (crushed, filled, happened) ✔ -ed with base change (died, excited, exploded, named, placed, raced, sized, slammed, spotted, tugged) ✔ y as a vowel (by, fly, gravity, sky, study, system)	expert *(experto/a)* follow gravity *(gravedad)* orbit *(órbita)* telescope *(telescopio)*	damage, experts, follow, form, formed, move, need, powerful, ready, reasons, scientists, simple, system, universe
(20) **The Champ and Other Stories** LEXILE 270	classic retelling	✔ Suffixes -y and -ly (angrily, dizzily, funny, fuzzy, gladly, grumpy, happily, instantly, messy, quickly, rapidly) ✔ Change y to i (angrily, dizzily, happily, tries)	boring challenge contest enjoy instant *(instante)* trick	challenge, counted, machine, moved
(21) **From the Heart** LEXILE 280	science	✔ Silent letters (wrapped, wrist, wrote) ✔ ph (phone) ✔ Digraph wh- (when, which, whipped, whisked) ✔ Review inflectional endings -ed, -ing (acted, checking, dressed, happened, hoping, landed, placed, pumping, struggling, telling, thinking, visited, whisked, wrapped)	donate *(donar)* infection *(infección)* reject severe surgery *(cirugía)* survive *(sobrevivir)*	acted, acting, arrived, body, charge, decide, family, machine, needed, operating, patient, patients, raised, severe, severely, struggling, survive, survived, treat, true, type, united
(22) **The Mummy King** LEXILE 250	social studies	✔ Open syllables (broken, finally, items, located, moment, opened, stolen) ✔ Unstressed open syllables (adult, ago, became, magnificent)	kingdom magnificent *(magnífico/a)* mummy *(momia)* rule temple *(templo)* tomb *(tumba)*	became, body, entered, located, need, prepared, rule, ruled

Title	Genre	Phonics Focus	Smart Words (With Spanish Cognates)	General Academic Words
23 **Disaster!** LEXILE 330	science	✔ *com-* and *con-* (combined, common, completely, computed, concrete, construct, contacted, contributed, convinced)	**aid** **damage** **escape** *(escapar)* **massive** *(masivo)* **survivor** **warning**	aid, compared, damage, damaged, decided, deliver, destroyed, determined, family, followed, form, formed, level, moving, natural, needed, objects, occurred, power, produced, protect, reached, remained, result, ruins, supposed, survive, united, unnatural, unprotected, warning
24 **In Search of the Giant Squid** LEXILE 350	science	✔ Long *a* vowel teams *ai* and *ay* (afraid, away, bait, claim, day, may, paid, remain, sailing, say, tail, waited, way)	**creature** *(criatura)* **exist** *(existir)* **huge** **locate** *(localizar)* **squid** **unusual** *(inusual— closer to "uncommon" than to "strange" or "extraordinary")*	amazed, amazing, attack, attacking, become, body, captured, claim, creature, dangerous, decided, disappeared, equipment, exist, expected, group, groups, locate, means, move, moved, moving, needed, offers, person, photographs, reach, scientist, scientists, struggle, struggled, true, type, unusual
25 **Mookie Is Missing!** LEXILE 330	fiction	✔ Long *o* vowel teams *oa* and *ow* (approached, boasted, below, blow, groaned, grown, Joan, know, load, moaned, own, pillow, road, show, Sloan, throw, Willow, window)	**apartment** *(apartamento)* **director** *(director/a)* **gorilla** *(gorila)* **noise** **occur** *(ocurrir)* **zoo** *(zoológico)*	approached, director, exciting, experiment, figured, guard, guards, needed, noticed, offered, reached, scientist, supposed, true
26 **Samurai Fighters** LEXILE 300	social studies	✔ Long *e* vowel teams *ea*, *ee*, and *ie* (beat, defeat, disagree, each, easy, free, greedy, keep, means, need, piece, pleaded, read, see, sneak, teaches, team, thieves, three, weak)	**clan** *(clan)* **defeat** **emperor** *(emperador)* **enemy** *(enemigo /a)* **legend** *(leyenda)* **samurai** *(samurai)*	became, defeat, disagree, enemies, enemy, expert, former, less, loyal, mean, means, need, needed, power, powerful, practice, prepares, respect, respected, rule, ruled, serve, served, sign, special, true
27 **The Lost City** LEXILE 340	social studies	✔ Prefixes *pre-* and *re-* (precut, predates, preshaped, refind, regain, remade) ✔ Long *i igh* (fight, sight, tightly) ✔ Other long *i* spelling *ild, ind* (wild, behind, find) ✔ Other long *o* spellings (gold, jolted, old, told)	**ancient** **empire** *(imperio)* **reveal** *(revelar)* **ruins** *(ruinas)* **site** *(sitio—general word for "place," does not specifically mean "archeological site")* **structure** *(estructura)*	achievement, amazing, connected, customs, decide, disagree, disappear, discovered, enemies, excited, exist, experts, explorers, group, important, means, mystery, nation, powerful, reached, reveal, revealed, ruins, ruled, structures, travel
28 **Narrative of the Life of Frederick Douglass** LEXILE 260	graphic novel/classic retelling	✔ Multiple affixes (misbehaving, returned) ✔ Ending *-ed* with base change (arrived, begged, carried, cried, decided, escaped, grabbed, realized, refused, stopped, tied, tried, whipped) ✔ Review suffix *-ly* (deeply, finally, slowly)	**cruel** *(cruel)* **force** **freedom** **illegal** *(ilegal)* **refuse** **slavery**	act, arrived, body, crime, dangerous, decided, destroy, equal, illegal, master, moved, nervous, ready, realized, refused, relative

LEXILE RANGE 200 – 350

Library Overview Lexile range 300–450

Title	Genre	Phonics Focus	Smart Words (With Spanish Cognates)	General Academic Words
(29) Killer Croc LEXILE 430	science	✔ *r-* controlled vowels *ar, er, ir,* and *ur* (better, car, expert, far, first, hard, large, monster, November, number, return, river, scars, smart, survivors) ✔ Suffixes *-er* and *-or* (hunters, killer, ranger, survivors, swimmers)	**capture** *(capturar)* **dangerous** **expose** *(exponer)* **fail** **reptile** *(reptil)* **risk** **terror** *(terror)*	attacked, attacking, attacks, body, capture, captured, choice, collects, dangerous, decided, disappeared, disappears, enter, entered, excited, expert, experts, figured, follow, includes, less, moved, need, needed, polluted, possible, ranger, respect, scientist, sense, sign, truth, view
(30) Dance Fever LEXILE 420	social studies	✔ *r-*controlled vowel *or, ore* (before, born, forever, form, more, New York, normal, perform, Shorty, story, torn, wore) ✔ */sh/* spellings *ci* and *ti* (competition, destination, inspiration, introduction, invention, magician, motivation, musician, nation, special, tradition)	**compete** *(competir)* **destination** *(destino)* **inspire** *(inspirar)* **partner** **perform** **rhythm** *(ritmo)* **tradition** *(tradición)*	amazing, appeared, arrived, became, body, borrowed, choice, circle, competed, competition, creating, decided, discovered, entered, exciting, exercise, express, expressed, expression, family, follow, form, government, group, groups, invent, invented, inventing, invention, less, moved, moves, nation, normal, needed, perform, performed, performing, purpose, ruled, rules, special, strict, tradition, united, usually
(31) Weird Science Jobs LEXILE 430	jobs	✔ *r-*controlled vowels *-are, -air,* and *-ear* (air, aware, bear, care, compares, dare, hair, prepare, scared, share, tear) ✔ Suffixes *-er* and *-est* (darker, deeper, faster, fastest, happiest, older, slower)	**investigate** *(investigar)* **reason** *(razón)* **scientist** *(científico/a)* **search** **solve** *(resolver)* **study** *(estudiar)* **theory** *(teoría)*	action, became, body, compared, compares, curve, detective, director, energy, enjoy, equipment, examines, explains, family, figure, investigating, matter, mysteries, mystery, need, needed, notice, power, prepare, prepared, raise, reason, ruled, science, scientist, scientists, solve, solved, solves, solving, special, survive, theory, treat, view
(32) Sky Walkers LEXILE 440	social studies	✔ Diphthongs *oi, ou, ow,* and *oy* (boys, broiling, choices, destroyed, hoist, joined, joyful, toil) ✔ Diphthongs *ou* and *ow* (about, around, clouds, doubt, down, found, ground, how, now, out, pounds, proud, towers) ✔ Suffixes *-ful* and *-less* (careful, careless, fearless, hopeful, joyful, skillful, stressful, tireless)	**balance** *(balancear—more commonly used as "to sway," but can mean "to balance")* **community** *(comunidad)* **construct** *(construir)* **project** *(proyecto)* **rubble** **success** **vertical** *(vertical)*	agrees, attacks, balance, became, become, challenge, center, choices, connected, connecting, connects, construct, construction, continue, course, dangerous, decide, decisions, design, designed, destroyed, difficult, encouraged, equipment, extreme, extremely, family, group, include, move, moved, moving, need, needed, object, project, ready, situation, structures, support, threat, threats, trade, tradition, true, united, usually, view

Title	Genre	Phonics Focus	Smart Words (With Spanish Cognates)	General Academic Words
33 **War of the Worlds** * LEXILE 260	graphic novel/ classic retelling	✔ *oo* and *ew* (cooler, crews, doomed, flew, food, foolish, grew, knew, looted, moon, news, room, shoot, soon, too) ✔ Prefixes *mid-*, *pre-*, and *sub-* (midmorning, midnight, predict, suburbs, subways) ✔ Roots *dict* and *port* (predict, transport, report)	crater *(cráter)* disturbing explode *(explotar)* Martian *(marciano/a)* meteor *(meteoro)* planet *(planeta)* universe *(universo)*	act, arrived, capture, charge, course, creatures, decided, destroyed, disturbing, enemy, machine, means, need, needed, possible, predict, predicting, predictions, reached, realize, refused, report, sign, simple, survive, survived, transport, true, universe, warn
34 **Everyday Heroes** LEXILE 440	social studies	✔ *oo* and *u* (book, Brooklyn, foot, good, hook, looked, misunderstood, onlookers, pull, pushing, put, shook, stood, took, wool) ✔ Prefixes *dis-* and *mis-* (disable, discover, discovery, misunderstood) ✔ Roots *rupt*, *struct*, and *scrib/script* (abruptly, construction, describe, instructed, instructions, interrupted, script)	discovery distract *(distraer)* distress hesitate instruct *(instruir)* maneuver *(maniobra)* station *(estación)*	able, act, acting, action, appeared, approached, arrived, attack, attacked, balance, body, certain, charge, collection, construction, counter, crime, curve, danger, decided, disappeared, discover, discovery, discussed, disturbing, enjoyed, family, followed, gently, ignored, instructions, less, location, matter, mattered, meant, memorial, move, moving, need, needed, nervous, nervousness, noticed, occurred, offered, perform, possibility, protect, reached, recalling, received, rule, serving, signs, solid, struggled, survive, united, unusual, unusually
35 **Fun Body Facts** LEXILE 430	science	✔ *a*, *au*, and *aw* (all, also, applaud, awful, called, cause, falls, fault, raw, salt, swallow, talk) ✔ Suffixes *-sion* and *-tion* (combination, conclusion, confusion, expression, motion, perspiration, reaction) ✔ Roots *auto*, *bio*, and *graph* (automatic, biology, photographs)	bacteria *(bacteria)* cell *(célula)* digest *(digerir)* healthy normal *(normal)* produce *(producir)* react *(reaccionar)*	able, apply, arrive, arrives, body, combination, confused, contain, contains, contents, course, dangerous, decides, exercise, flows, follow, form, important, less, means, moving, need, nervous, normal, person, prevent, prevents, process, produce, produced, produces, protect, protects, ready, reason, reasons, remember, result, sign, signal, signals, special, type, types, usually
36 **The Legend of Sleepy Hollow** LEXILE 320	classic retelling	✔ Prefix *tri-* (triangle) ✔ Suffixes *-able* and *-ible* (adorable, enjoyable, possible, respectable, sensible, unbearable, unbelievable) ✔ Roots *scope*, *tele*, and *vis/vid* (envisioned, microscope, telescope, vision, visited)	comfortable coward *(cobarde)* haunted impress *(impresionar)* panic *(pánico)* terrible *(terrible)* vanish	agrees, amazed, body, choose, comfortable, educated, enjoyable, family, follow, impress, impressed, move, moved, possible, reach, reached, ready, remember, respectable, sign, solve, surround, wandered

LEXILE RANGE 300 – 450

* Graphic novels may fall out of Lexile range.

Why Use Decoding Routines?

- These routines help students match sounds with the symbols used to represent them in words.
- Orally blending words helps students decode words while reading.
- Decoding skills lead to rapid word recognition, greater fluency, and improved comprehension.
- As students develop decoding skills, they become more able to devote their full attention to making meaning from text.

Purpose

Recognizing syllable patterns helps students correctly determine vowel sounds and decode unfamiliar words.

Decoding Routines

Use these brief and playful routines with books in the System 44 Library to help students grasp sound-symbol relationships.

Use these routines to provide fast-paced support. To maximize benefits to students be sure to:

- Repeat tasks as often as necessary until students demonstrate success.
- Modify tasks to help students who demonstrate difficulty.
- Informally monitor students during decoding routines and select those who need additional intervention.
- Provide additional support as needed by backtracking to an easier step or providing more cues and examples.

Syllable Strategies

Guide students to read and write multisyllabic words with open and closed syllables.

1 Have students write the Phonics Focus words from the book on a piece of paper. Review key syllable concepts, including:

- Every syllable has just one vowel sound.
- Syllables that end in a consonant are called closed syllables and usually have a short vowel sound.
- Syllables that end in a vowel are called open syllables and usually have a long vowel sound.

2 Guide students to use the Look, Spot, Split, and Read strategy to analyze and read the words. This strategy is available in the *44Book*, page 184, for students' reference.

Look for any prefixes, suffixes, or endings you know.
- Remember, the spelling of the base word may have changed when the ending or suffix was added.

Spot the vowels in the base word. The number of vowel spots tells the number of syllables.
- Remember, some vowel sounds are spelled with more than one letter.

Split the word into syllables.
- A good place to split a word is between two consonants.
- If there is only one consonant between syllables, try splitting after it.

Read the word. Does it make a real word? If not, you may need to split the word in a different place or try using a different vowel sound.

Syllable Type Examples

Book	Syllable Type	Phonics Focus Words
Book 7: *Mystery Photo*	Closed Syllables	baskets, biggest, contest, hidden, invent, linen, napkin, objects, panic, sunset, traffic
Book 13: *Button Your Lip and Other Idioms*	Closed Syllables With Schwa	button, common, finish, gossip, happens, jacket, kitchen, kitten, piglets, problem
Book 14: *African Journey*	Consonant + *-al*, *-el*, or *-le*	animals, cattle, jungle, little, mammals, middle, rental, simple, single, travel
Book 22: *The Mummy King*	Open Syllables	broken, finally, items, located, moment, opened, stolen
	Unstressed Open Syllables	adult, ago, became, magnificent

Blends and Digraphs

Guide students to recognize common consonant blends and digraphs.

1 Write a list of words on the board or on a piece of paper, some with consonant blends and some with consonant digraphs, and have students copy the words. Try to pick a sampling of words that shows blends and digraphs in the beginning, middle, and end positions. (Check the charts below for possible examples.)

2 Explain that a consonant blend is two or more consonants that appear together in a word, with each retaining its own sound. Point out an example from the list of words.

3 Explain that a consonant digraph is two consonants that stand for one sound, such as *ch*, *sh*, and *th*. Point out an example from the list of words.

4 Ask students to read each word on the list, circle the consonant blends, and underline the digraphs.

Purpose

Recognition of digraphs and familiarity with common consonant blends leads to improved decoding and automaticity.

Blends Examples

Book	Phonics Focus Words
Book 3: *Sports Bloopers*	scab, skill, skip, slam, slip, snaps, sped, spell, spot, stands, step, stop
Book 4: *Fast! The World's Fastest Couch and Other Fast Things*	blast, brisk, desk, fast, glad, grip, must, plan, plant, rest, risk, sprigs, strap, trip, twigs, twins
Book 5: *I Do Not Eat Worms (and Other Poems)*	sink
Book 6: *Wonders of the World*	act, gift, help, lift, plants, ramp, send, sent, stand, went

Digraphs Examples

Book	Phonics Focus Words
Book 5: *I Do Not Eat Worms (and Other Poems)*	sing
Book 8: *Travels With Mapman*	crash, dash, finish, fish, gash, gushes, mash, rush, shift, ships, shut, splash, wishes
Book 9: *The Gift*	bunch, check, Chet, ditch, hunch, lunch, match, much, rich, switch
Book 10: *Gross Bugs!*	path, thanks, that, them, then, thin, think, this, with
Book 11: *Signs*	batch, catch, check, match, shocking, Spanish, that, them, think, this
Book 21: *From the Heart*	when, which, whipped, whisked

Word Parts

Students identify and define prefixes, suffixes, inflectional endings, and roots.

Prefixes

1. Review with students that a prefix is a word part that can be added to the beginning of a base word to change its meaning. *For example, the prefix* mis- *means "wrong." The word* misunderstood *means that someone has understood wrongly or incorrectly.*

2. Ask students to list words with prefixes from their current Paperback, leaving room to write beneath each word. Then, ask them to write out the prefix and base word as an addition problem for each word. For example, the word *misunderstood* would be written as follows: *mis- + understood = misunderstood.*

3. Ask students to read each word part separately and then put the parts together to read the whole word.

Prefixes Examples

Book	Prefix	Phonics Focus Words
Book 17: *Cool Jobs in Basketball*	*non-* *un-*	nonathletes, nonstop, unexpected, unpacks
Book 23: *Disaster!*	*com-* *con-*	combined, common, completely, computed, concrete, construct, contacted, contributed, convinced
Book 27: *The Lost City*	*pre-* *re-*	precut, predates, preshaped, refind, regain, remade
Book 28: *Narrative of the Life of Frederick Douglass*	*mis-* *re-*	misbehaving, returned
Book 33: *War of the Worlds*	*mid-* *pre-* *sub-*	midmorning, midnight, predict, suburbs, subways
Book 34: *Everyday Heroes*	*dis-* *mis-*	disable, discover, discovery, misunderstood
Book 36: *The Legend of Sleepy Hollow*	*tri-*	triangle

Purpose

Recognizing common word parts helps students decode multisyllabic words with greater automaticity. Knowing the meanings of word parts helps students to determine the meanings of unfamiliar words in context.

This routine is best used to practice prefixes, suffixes, inflectional endings, and roots.

Suffixes and Inflectional Endings

1 Explain that suffixes are word parts that can be added to the end of a base word to change the word's meaning or part of speech. *For example, the suffix* -ful *means "full of." The word* hopeful *means "full of hope." Adding* -ful *to the noun* hope *created the adjective* hopeful. Explain that inflectional endings may make a noun plural, change the tense of a verb, or help a verb agree with its subject.

2 Ask students to list words with suffixes or endings from their current book, leaving room to write beneath each word. Then, ask them to write out the base word and suffix or ending as a math equation for each word. For example, the word *hopeful* would be written as follows: *hope + -ful = hopeful.*

Note: Remind students that adding suffixes or endings to some base words requires spelling changes. Help them include these changes in their equations (for example: *happy – y + i + -ness = happiness; nice – e + -er = nicer; big + g + -est = biggest*). For words with suffixes *-tion, -sion, -able,* and *-ible,* ask students to divide the word into syllables, then create an equation by adding the syllables and suffix or ending (for example: *ac + -tion = action; un- + pre- + dict + -able = unpredictable*).

3 Ask students to read each word part separately and then put the parts together to form the whole word.

Suffixes Examples

Book	Suffix	Phonics Focus Words
Book 16: *Win or Lose?*	-ment -ness	equipment, statement, sadness
Book 20: *The Champ and Other Stories*	-y -ly	angrily, dizzily, funny, fuzzy, gladly, grumpy, happily, instantly, messy, quickly, rapidly
Book 28: *Narrative of the Life of Frederick Douglass*	-ly	deeply, finally, slowly
Book 29: *Killer Croc*	-er -or	hunters, killer, ranger, survivors, swimmers
Book 31: *Weird Science Jobs*	-er -est	darker, deeper, faster, fastest, happiest, older, slower
Book 32: *Sky Walkers*	-ful -less	careful, careless, fearless, hopeful, joyful, skillful, stressful, tireless
Book 35: *Fun Body Facts*	-sion -tion	combination, conclusion, confusion, expression, motion, perspiration, reaction
Book 36: *The Legend of Sleepy Hollow*	-able -ible	adorable, enjoyable, possible, respectable, sensible, unbearable, unbelievable

RULES TO KNOW: Suffixes and Endings

Rule 1

VC + ending that begins with a vowel = double the final consonant

EXPLANATION: When a word ends with a short vowel followed by a single consonant, double the final consonant before adding a suffix or ending that begins with a vowel *(hopped, running, muddy).*

Rule 2

silent *e* + ending that begins with a vowel = drop the silent *e*

EXPLANATION: When a word ends with a silent *e*, drop the *e* before adding a suffix or ending that starts with a vowel *(racing, finer).*

Rule 3

consonant-*y* + ending that begins with a vowel = change *y* to *i* (except *-ing*)

EXPLANATION: When a word ends with a consonant and *y*, change the *y* to *i* before adding a suffix or ending that starts with a vowel, except for *-ing* *(dutiful, luckily, muddier, dried, babies, crying).*

ADDITIONAL ROOTS FOR INSTRUCTION

Greek Roots

hydro (water)

meter (measure)

ology (word or study)

photo (light)

therm (heat)

EXAMPLES

hydrogen, hydroplane
thermometer, perimeter
geology, zoology
photography, photocopy
thermometer, thermos

Latin Roots

aud (to hear)

ject (to throw)

tract (to draw or pull)

EXAMPLES

audience, audio
reject, inject, eject
tractor, attract, extract

Anglo-Saxon Roots

kno (skill)

lik (similar, to be pleased with)

tru (faithful)

EXAMPLES

know, knowledge, knew
like, likeness, likely
truth, true, truly

Inflectional Endings Examples

Book	Inflectional Ending	Phonics Focus Words
Book 2: *Messy Jobs*	-s -es	bits, cuts, digs, dips, fixes, gets, lots, mixes, rocks, rots, wins
Book 11: *Signs*	-ing with no base change	bending, ending, happening, helping, shocking, telling
Book 12: *Fashion Flashback*	-ed with no base change	acted, blasted, dressed, ended, expected, fixed, instructed, jazzed, lasted, lifted, limited, matched, missed, packed, shifted, shocked, stacked, stomped, tricked, wished
Book 18: *Meet the Dragon Slayers*	-ing	killing, shocking
	-ing with base change	running, saving, zipping
Book 19: *Crash!*	-ed with no base change	crushed, filled, happened
	-ed with base change	died, excited, exploded, named, placed, raced, sized, slammed, spotted, tugged
Book 20: *The Champ and Other Stories*	-es	tries
Book 21: *From the Heart*	-ed and -ing	acted, checking, dressed, happened, hoping, landed, placed, pumping, struggling, telling, thinking, visited, whisked, wrapped
Book 28: *Narrative of the Life of Frederick Douglass*	-ed and -ing	misbehaving, returned

Roots

Remind students that many words in the English language come from Greek, Latin and Anglo-Saxon roots. *Knowing the meaning of roots can help you figure out the meanings of words you don't know. For example, the root* tele *means "far off," and the root* scope *means "to see." A telescope lets you see things that are far away.*

Ask students to list words with roots from their current book. Then, ask them to circle all of the roots they can find in each word. Guide students to explain how the root of each word contributes to the word's meaning. Students should use dictionaries as needed.

Roots Examples

Book	Root Words	Phonics Focus Words
Book 33: *War of the Worlds*	*dict, port*	predict, transport, report
Book 34: *Everyday Heroes*	*rupt, struct, scrib/script*	abruptly, construction, describe, instructed, instructions, interrupted, script
Book 35: *Fun Body Facts*	*auto, bio, graph*	automatic, biology, photographs
Book 36: *The Legend of Sleepy Hollow*	*scope, tele, vis/vid*	envisioned, microscope, telescope, vision, visited

Word Sort

Guide students to practice putting familiar words into groups according to their sounds and/or spellings.

This routine can be used with most Phonics Focus elements. The example below uses Phonics Focus words with *r*-controlled vowels from Book 29, *Killer Croc*.

Have students use the Word Sort graphic organizer on **page 102** to sort the Phonics Focus words *better, car, expert, far, first, hard, large, monster, November, number, return, river, scars, smart,* and *survivors* into groups according to their vowel spellings: *ar, ir, er, ur, or.*

Ask students to identify a pattern or principle that is operating and state it aloud. For example, students may conclude that there are three ways to spell the /ûr/ sound as seen in the words *experts, return,* and *first.*

Purpose

Word sorting enhances visual and auditory attention to the internal details of words, and helps students remember correct spellings for words with vowel sounds that can be spelled more than one way.

This routine works with a variety of Phonics Focus elements.

Why Use Vocabulary/Word Study Routines?

- These routines give students tools they can use to understand and build vocabulary as they read.
- Vocabulary is fundamental to comprehension. Students cannot understand text without knowing what most of the words mean.
- Having a wide vocabulary is beneficial in building comprehension, as well as overall academic success.

Purpose

Students who practice reading words from different morphological families are more likely to notice familiar base words in longer words.

Associating words with synonyms and antonyms helps students build a larger vocabulary and develop reasoning skills.

Vocabulary/Word Study Routines

Use these routines to help your students build vocabulary.

These routines will equip students with strategies for unlocking unfamiliar words and building vocabulary as they read.

Extending Meaning

Guide students to look for connections among words with the same base, root, or meaning.

Morphological Word Families

Have students write an appropriate Smart Word on a piece of paper. Guide students to notice if the word is formed from a base word, or whether it is a base word itself. Work together to create a list of other words with the same base. For example, the following words share the base *present*: *represent*, *presentation*, *misrepresent*, and *presentable*. Discuss how the base word relates to the meaning of each word.

For words with familiar Greek or Latin roots, ask students to come up with words they know that use the root. For example, the word *telescope* includes the root *tele*, meaning "far off." This root is shared with the words *television*, *telephone*, and *telegraph*. Discuss how the root contributes to the meaning of each word.

Discuss how identifying a familiar word part or base can help students figure out the meaning of an unfamiliar word as they read.

Examples

Book	Smart Word	Word Family
Book 1: *Hunt and Kill*	attack	attacked, attacking, attacker, attacks
Book 5: *I Do Not Eat Worms (and Other Poems)*	express	expressed, expressing, expression, expressions, expressive
Book 7: *Mystery Photo*	invent	invented, inventing, invention, inventions, inventive, inventor
Book 11: *Signs*	sign	signal, signaled, signaling, signals, signed, signing, signs
Book 13: *Button Your Lip and Other Idioms*	explain	explained, unexplained, explaining, explains, explainable, unexplainable, explanation, explanatory
Book 25: *Mookie Is Missing!*	director	direct, directed, directing, direction, directions, directly, directors, directs
Book 31: *Weird Science Jobs*	scientist	science, scientists, sciences, scientific, scientifically
Book 34: *Everyday Heroes*	discovery	discover, discovered, discoveries, discovering, discovers
Book 36: *The Legend of Sleepy Hollow*	comfortable	comfort, comfortably, comforted, comforting, comforts, discomfort

Synonyms and Antonyms

Have students write an appropriate Smart Word on a piece of paper. (See the chart below for suggestions). Challenge students to make a list of as many synonyms (words with similar meanings) and antonyms (words with opposite meanings) as they can think of, with the aid of a thesaurus if necessary.

Examples

Book	Smart Word	Possible Synonyms	Possible Antonyms
Book 17: *Cool Jobs in Basketball*	rely	trust, have faith in, depend on, count on	distrust, doubt, question
Book 23: *Disaster!*	aid	help, assist, relieve, support, back	hurt, block, harm, injure
Book 29: *Killer Croc*	dangerous	risky, unsafe, hazardous, perilous, threatening	safe, harmless, secure, protected

Multiple-Meaning Words

Guide students to learn to use context to help determine the correct meaning for multiple-meaning words.

1 **Define Multiple-Meaning Words** Tell students that some words have more than one meaning. To figure out a word's meaning, readers must use clues from the sentence or from surrounding sentences.

2 **Identify Multiple-Meaning Words** Introduce students to a multiple-meaning word, and provide at least two alternate meanings. Present the word in context by reading the sentence or sentences in which it appears, and then think aloud to demonstrate how you determine which meaning best fits the context.

The following example uses the multiple-meaning word *rule* from page 7 of Book 22, *The Mummy King*:

Read the second full paragraph aloud. Tell students that the word *rule* has multiple meanings. *Rule* can mean "to have power over something" or "a law." *The context clue "too young to rule a kingdom" helps me realize that King Tut has power over Egypt.*

3 **Practice** Ask students to use each meaning of the multiple-meaning word in an oral sentence.

Purpose

Knowledge of multiple-meaning words helps students develop strategies for identifying correct word meaning, to build text comprehension.

Examples of Smart Words With Multiple Meanings

Book	Page and Paragraph	Smart Word	Meanings
Book 2: *Messy Jobs*	Page 3, paragraph 3	waste	"to throw something away before it's used" or "garbage"
Book 6: *Wonders of the World*	Page 3, paragraph 1	wonder	"something that's amazing or surprising" or "to be curious about something"
Book 8: *Travels With Mapman*	Page 7, paragraph 1	coast	"land next to a body of water" or "to drift, float, or glide"
Book 10: *Gross Bugs!*	Page 8, paragraph 3	type	"kind or sort" or "to write using a keyboard"
Book 15: *Ripped From the Headlines*	Page 4, paragraph 1	brave	"not afraid" or "to do something difficult," as in "He braved the storm."
Book 19: *Crash!*	Page 7, bottom paragraph	follow	"to watch or keep track of something" or "to chase or pursue"
Book 20: *The Champ and Other Stories*	Page 8, paragraph 1	trick	"a stunt or skillful move" or "to fool or cheat someone"
Book 22: *The Mummy King*	Page 7, paragraph 3	rule	"to have power over something" or "a law"
Book 27: *The Lost City*	Page 13, paragraph 3	structure	"something that has been built" or "the way something is put together"

Context Clues

Students learn strategies to determine the meaning of unfamiliar words based on their context.

1 **Define Context Clues** Explain that when they come across an unfamiliar word, students can sometimes figure out what it means by looking for clues from other words or sentences around it.

2 **Identify Context Clues** Introduce a Smart Word students are unfamiliar with, and then read the sentence or paragraph (as needed) in which it appears. Ask students to listen for any words that may shed light on the meaning of the unknown Smart Word. Model how to use context clues by thinking aloud for students.

This example uses the Smart Word *migrate* from page 8 of Book 14, *African Journey*:

I'll read the last paragraph aloud. As I read, I will look for clues in the text that help me figure out the meaning of the word migrate.

Explain that the phrase *travel really far* suggests that *migrate* means "to move from one country or region to another."

Explain that students need to reread to confirm their ideas. If students find a definition does not fit the context, they should try again or consult a dictionary.

Purpose

Using context clues helps students determine the meanings of unfamiliar words in context, increasing their comprehension and confidence.

3 Practice Ask students to use the Vocabulary Builder graphic organizer on **page 103** to jot down unfamiliar words they encounter as they read. Have students first attempt to use context clues to figure out the meaning of each word. Next, ask them to look up the word in the dictionary and compare how closely their definition matches the dictionary definition. Finally, have students record the dictionary definition in the Vocabulary Builder.

Examples of Context Clues

Book	Page and Paragraph	Smart Word	Context Clues
Book 14: *African Journey*	Page 8, paragraph 2	migrate	Some animals migrate.... Wildebeests travel really far.
Book 21: *From the Heart*	Page 8, paragraph 4	donate	Texans raised money.... People donated half a million dollars.
Book 24: *In Search of the Giant Squid*	Page 9, paragraph 2	creature	The sailors decided to catch the creature. They wrapped a rope around its tail.
Book 26: *Samurai Fighters*	Page 12, paragraph 2	legend	One samurai woman became a legend... People said she could not be defeated.
Book 30: *Dance Fever*	Page 6, paragraph 2	tradition	You can follow tradition. You can dance the way your grandparents did.
Book 33: *War of the Worlds*	Page 8, last panel	meteor	It must be a meteor shower. The meteors are hitting Mars and causing the flames.
Book 35: *Fun Body Facts*	Page 16, paragraph 1	bacteria	The average mouth is home to 10 billion bacteria!

Idioms

Students learn to identify and understand the meaning of idioms.

1 Define Idioms Tell students that an *idiom* is a phrase or expression that has a meaning that is different from the literal or actual meaning of the words.

2 Identify Idioms Ask students to listen as you read a passage aloud. Identify the idiom for students and explain its meaning, pointing out how the literal meaning of the words is different from the meaning of the expression.

This example uses the idiom *paid off* from page 16 of Book 18, *Meet the Dragon Slayers*:

I'll read the second to last paragraph aloud. As I read, listen for the idiom "paid off." Explain to students that the expression *paid off* means "resulted in success."

3 Practice Have students use the idiom in at least one oral sentence.

Purpose

This routine is particularly helpful for students who are new to English, as they may not be familiar with the idiomatic meaning of an expression.

Why Use Fluency Routines?

- Repeated oral reading with teacher feedback builds fluency and improves comprehension.

- Fluency routines provide varied and engaging ways for students to focus on the qualities of fluent reading.

- The use of routines provides an efficient and familiar way to incorporate regular fluency practice into the classroom.

Student Objectives

- Read aloud fluently, with appropriate tone, phrasing, pacing, and expression.

Fluency Routines

Fluency helps students focus on the purpose of reading—extracting and constructing meaning.

Fluency in the Classroom

Timothy Rasinski, a fluency expert and professor of education, defines fluency as, "the ability to read quickly, effortlessly, and efficiently with good, meaningful expression." These routines promote fluency by providing practice exercises to support correct phrasing, speed, and expression.

To create meaningful contexts and authentic purposes for fluency instruction and practice, make fluency routines a familiar and regular part of instruction. Give students daily opportunities to read aloud and to gain confidence. Help students see connections between fluent oral and fluent silent reading, and guide them in using fluency terms such as *expression, tone of voice,* and *phrasing.* Use fluency routines with suggested passages from books in the *System 44* Library, or choose your own passages. Add your own ideas, combine methods, and discover the routines that work best for you.

Phrasing and Punctuation

Students learn to read fluently by "chunking" text, making appropriate pauses, and varying their tone.

1 **Explain Correct Phrasing** Explain that phrases are groups of words, or "chunks" of text, that go together to make meaning. Fluent readers read in meaningful phrases. Point out that reading with good phrasing helps make text's meaning clear. Briefly discuss the following qualities of phrasing.

- **Pause** Make a slight pause between the parts of a sentence. Stop to take a breath when you see a comma between words. Pause at the end of a sentence.

- **Express the meaning** Stress some words more than others. Raise or lower the tone of your voice. Read some phrases faster or slower. Express excitement when you see an exclamation mark. Read sentences with question marks as questions.

- **Use Phrasing** Consider beginning a new phrase when you see prepositions such as *with, in, to, by, at, on,* and *for,* and transition words such as *then, next, and, but, or,* and *however.*

2 **Model Correct Phrasing** Distribute copies of the Fluency Checklist on **page 104**. Ask students to turn to the selected passages in their books and follow along as you read a paragraph. Read the paragraph in meaningful phrases, emphasizing and slightly exaggerating the phrases. Read with expression at a varied rate, and pause for punctuation.

Ask students to name one quality of fluency they heard in your reading. Have them refer to the Fluency Checklist. Return to the text and identify examples of your phrasing, pauses, emphasis, and expression. Make a check on the list for each quality as it is mentioned.

3 **Practice** Have students read through the passage and identify phrasing cues. They should identify punctuation cues, including commas, periods, question marks, and exclamation marks. They should also look for transition words such as *then, next, and, but, or,* and *however* and prepositions such as *with, in, to, by, at, on,* and *for.* Lastly, ask them to choose a few key words that may be important to stress because of meaning.

For partnered reading, ask students to take turns reading the passage while others listen and fill out the Fluency Checklist. Students who listened should then offer constructive feedback about successes and areas for improvement.

For independent practice, have students use a tape recorder to listen to and to evaluate their reading as they reread the passage, experimenting with different pauses, word stresses, and reading speeds. Offer constructive feedback as needed.

Suggested Passages for Practicing Correct Phrasing

Book	Passage
Book 2: *Messy Jobs*	Pages 4–5
Book 7: *Mystery Photo*	Pages 4–5
Book 12: *Fashion Flashback*	Pages 10–11
Book 14: *African Journey*	Pages 8–11
Book 17: *Cool Jobs in Basketball*	Pages 8–9
Book 35: *Fun Body Facts*	Page 6

Use Natural, Consistent Pace

Students read and reread for skill, pacing, and accuracy.

1 **Explain Pacing** Briefly discuss how practice makes everything easier—from sports to playing an instrument to cooking. *When people train or rehearse, they practice the same moves, steps, or notes over and over again. Reading is also a skill that can be improved through practice.*

Point out that the best way to make reading automatic is to practice reading the same words again and again. Explain to students that they will practice by reading the same passage several times. Each time they reread the passage, they will begin to recognize more words automatically and will be able to read at a more comfortable pace. They will measure this progress by seeing how much of the passage they can read in one minute. Emphasize that the goal is not to race through the passage, but to read it fluently.

Student Objectives

- Read and reread for speed and accuracy.
- Master unfamiliar words in passages.
- Track fluency progress.

2 **Model Correct Pacing** Ask students to turn to the selected passages in their books. Tell students that you will be timing yourself to see how much of the passage you can read in one minute. Give one student a stopwatch and ask him or her to let you know when one minute is up. Explain that you will be reading for accuracy as well as speed. Ask students to follow along in their books as you read. They should notice where you are at the end of one minute, and make note of any words you read incorrectly.

Read the passage at a natural pace. Read a few simple words incorrectly. Stop reading after a minute, and ask students to identify how many words you misread. Explain that the goal of the exercise is to make sure your pace is not too fast or too slow, and to read all of the words correctly.

3 **Practice** Distribute stopwatches to students. Ask students to read the passage silently several times until they feel comfortable with reading all of the words.

For groups of three, ask students to take turns reading the passage from their books. While one student is reading, the second should be timing the exercise, and the third should be noting errors and the last word read. Students who listened should then offer constructive feedback about successes and areas for improvement.

For independent practice, have students use a tape recorder to record their reading. They should then listen with a stop watch and make note of errors and the last word read. Periodically check up on their readings and offer constructive feedback as needed.

On subsequent days, provide repeated opportunities to practice the same passage.

Suggested Passages for Modeling Correct Pacing

Book	Passage
Book 4: *Fast! The World's Fastest Couch and Other Fast Things*	Pages 3–5
Book 6: *Wonders of the World*	Pages 3–5
Book 15: *Ripped From the Headlines*	Pages 12–13
Book 18: *Meet the Dragon Slayers*	Pages 9–11
Book 26: *Samurai Fighters*	Pages 7–9
Book 34: *Everyday Heroes*	Pages 13–15

Read With Expression

Students learn to read in a varied, expressive tone.

1 **Explain Expressive Reading** Ask students to imagine that they are telling a story to their friends. *What are some things you would do to get your friend more interested in the story? Imagine you're telling a scary story. How would you tell it? Imagine you're telling a story about something funny that happened to you. Would you tell that story in the same way you tell a scary story?* Tell students that when they read out loud, it helps to imagine that they are telling a story to a friend and trying to get that friend interested in the story.

Explain that to read with expression, it helps to understand the story. So, before practicing expressive reading, they should read the entire story to understand what is happening in it.

2 **Model Expressive Reading** Ask students to turn to the selected passages in their books and follow along as you read. Read the passage twice. During the first reading, demonstrate how a reader's tone of voice and expression can show different feelings and reflect different characters. Ask students to describe your reading. For the second reading, read the passage flatly, without expression. Ask students to describe the difference.

3 **Practice** Ask students to read the selected text several times until they understand the story and feel comfortable reading all of the words.

For small group practice, distribute copies of the Fluency Checklist on **page 104**. Students should take turns with one reading while others listen and fill out the Fluency Checklist, with special attention paid to the Expression section. Students who listened should then offer constructive feedback about successes and areas for improvement.

For independent practice, have students use a tape recorder to listen to and to evaluate their reading as they reread the same passage, experimenting with varying emotions and emphasis. Offer constructive feedback as needed.

Suggested Passages for Practicing Expressive Reading

Book	Passage
Book 3: *Sports Bloopers*	Pages 4–5
Book 13: *Button Your Lip and Other Idioms*	Pages 10–12
Book 19: *Crash!*	Pages 10–11
Book 24: *In Search of the Giant Squid*	Page 10
Book 29: *Killer Croc*	Page 8
Book 36: *The Legend of Sleepy Hollow*	Pages 28–29

Purpose

- Rehearse to improve accuracy, phrasing, and prosody.
- Read for comprehension.
- Read to entertain.

Hunt and Kill: A Look at Predators
by **Rob Camacho**

Genre	Pages	Lexile	Audio CD	Reading
Science	**8**	**240**	**6 min 37 sec**	**Counts!**

Summary

Predators are animals that kill to eat. Owls have keen senses of sight and hearing to help them hunt. Crocodiles and sharks go after big prey. Jaguars use their strong bite to hunt at night in the jungle. The blue-ringed octopus poisons its prey to kill it. Survival is what causes these predators to hunt and kill.

Phonics Focus

- **Short vowels**
- **Consonants b, d, g, and p**

See **Master Skills Tracker:**
Teacher's Guide, page 548

Skills Tracker

Preteach   Teach/Practice/Apply   Review/Reinforce   Assess

Smart Words

Words are defined on p. 2 of the student book. Page number of first appearance is listed below.

- **attack***, p. 3
- **predator***, p. 3
- **prey**, p. 3

*Spanish Cognates, **page 10**

Option 1: **Decoding**

 Conference

Ask students to read the Phonics Focus words on the inside back cover of *Hunt and Kill*. If they struggle with decoding, proceed to individualized instruction.

 Individualized Instruction

For words with short vowels: Have students use the Word Sort decoding routine on **page 21** to sort words by their short vowel sounds.

For words with consonants b, d, g, and p: Have students use the Word Sort routine to sort words by consonant sounds.

Option 2: **Vocabulary**

 Conference

Ask students to use some Smart Words from the book in an oral sentence. Review definitions on page 2 as needed. If students demonstrate proficiency, proceed to individualized instruction.

 Individualized Instruction

The Smart Word *attack* is the base of the words *attacked, attacking, attacker,* and *attacks.* Use the **Extending Meaning** vocabulary routine on **page 22** to build student familiarity with morphological word families.

Option 3: **Fluency**

 Conference

Ask students to read page 3 of *Hunt and Kill* aloud. To work on correct phrasing, proceed to individualized instruction.

 Individualized Instruction

Use pages 3–5 of *Hunt and Kill* and the **Use Natural, Consistent Pace** fluency routine on **page 27** to have students practice reading at a natural pace.

Comprehension

Use the questions below and the Wrap-Up on **page 31** to check comprehension and promote reader response.

After Page 4: *How does a crocodile sneak up on its prey? (It quietly floats in the water like a log. Then it attacks.)*

End of Book: *Why does a blue-ringed octopus have two types of poison? (One kind protects the octopus from other predators. The other kind kills prey.)*

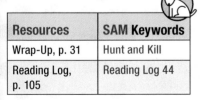

Resources	SAM **Keywords**
Wrap-Up, p. 31	Hunt and Kill
Reading Log, p. 105	Reading Log 44

Name _____

Hunt and Kill: A Look at Predators

Build Understanding

▶ Fill in the circles below with words or phrases that describe great white sharks. An example is done for you.

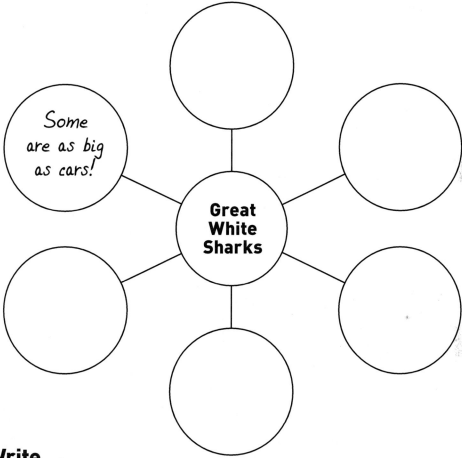

Some are as big as cars!

Great White Sharks

QuickWrite

▶ What makes great white sharks top predators? Support your answer with details from the book.

_____

_____

_____

Resource Links
Library Teaching Resources: p. 31
SAM Keyword: Hunt and Kill

Use with **Library Teaching Resources**, page 30.

Messy Jobs
by **Alan Takamura**

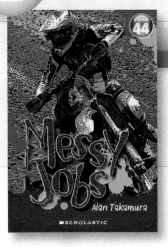

Genre	Pages	Lexile	Audio CD	Reading
Jobs	8	150	7 min 12 sec	Counts!

Summary

Some jobs are messy. Worm farmers dig up worms. Ship painters get covered in paint. Podiatrists handle feet. Clean-up workers mop up oil spills. Motocross bikers race through dirt. Read about the messes people in these jobs face at work.

Phonics Focus

- **Short vowels**
- *-s, -es*

See **Master Skills Tracker:** Teacher's Guide, page 548

Skills Tracker

Preteach | Teach/Practice/Apply | Review/Reinforce | Assess

Smart Words

Words are defined on p. 2 of the student book. Page number of first appearance is listed below.

- **machine*, p. 4**
- **stink, p. 3**
- **waste, p. 3**

*Spanish Cognates, **page 10**

Option 1: Decoding

 Conference

Ask students to read the Phonics Focus words on the inside back cover of *Messy Jobs.* If they struggle with decoding, proceed to individualized instruction.

 Individualized Instruction

For words with short vowels: Have students use the Word Sort decoding routine on **page 21** to sort words by their short vowel sounds.

For words with -s and -es: Use the Word Parts decoding routine on **page 18** to help students identify and use inflectional endings.

Option 2: Vocabulary

 Conference

Ask students to use some Smart Words listed on the inside back cover of *Messy Jobs* in an oral sentence. Review definitions on page 2 as needed. If students demonstrate proficiency, proceed to individualized instruction.

 Individualized Instruction

The Smart Word *waste* can mean "to throw something away before it's used" or "junk or garbage." Use the **Multiple-Meaning Words** vocabulary routine on **page 23** with *waste* as an example to help students use context to determine correct meaning.

Option 3: Fluency

 Conference

Ask students to read page 4 of *Messy Jobs* aloud. To work on reading with correct phrasing, proceed to individualized instruction.

 Individualized Instruction

Use pages 4–5 of *Messy Jobs* and the **Phrasing and Punctuation** fluency routine on **page 26** to have students practice correct phrasing.

Comprehension

Use the questions below and the Wrap-Up on **page 33** to check comprehension and promote reader response.

After Page 3: *What do farmers do with the worms and droppings? (They sell the worms as fishing bait. They sell the droppings as plant fertilizer.)*

After Page 5: *What is the job of a podiatrist? (A podiatrist's job is to take care of feet.)*

End of Book: *Why is motocross racing a messy job? (It's messy because racers ride in the dirt and get covered in mud.)*

Resources	SAM Keywords
Wrap-Up, p. 33	Messy Jobs
Reading Log, p. 105	Reading Log 44

Name _____

Messy Jobs

Build Understanding

▶ What would each person below say is the messiest part of his or her job? Write what each would say.

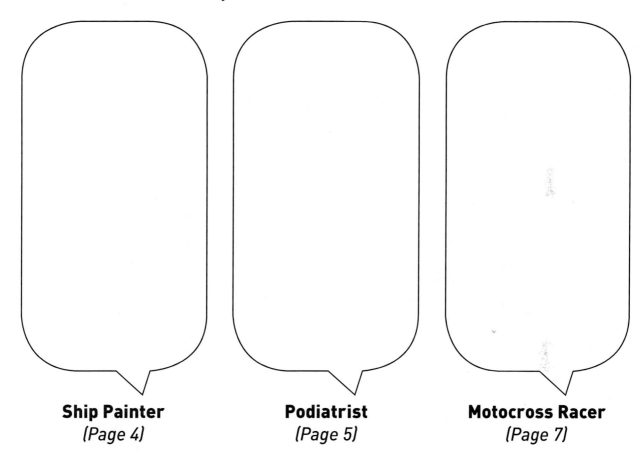

Ship Painter
(Page 4)

Podiatrist
(Page 5)

Motocross Racer
(Page 7)

QuickWrite

▶ Which messy job do you think is the most important? Why? Write a sentence that explains your opinion. Use details from the book to support your answer.

_____

_____

_____

Sports Bloopers
by **Peter Gutiérrez**

Genre	Pages	Lexile	Audio CD	Reading
Social Studies	**8**	**200**	**5 min 46 sec**	**Counts!**

Summary

Even great athletes make mistakes. The photographs in this book capture some classic bloopers, including a baseball player's cap slipping over his face, a basketball player flipping over a table, a gymnast falling off a beam, and other memorable moments.

Phonics Focus

- *s*- blends
- **Double consonants**

See **Master Skills Tracker:** Teacher's Guide, page 548

Skills Tracker

Preteach | Teach/Practice/Apply | Review/Reinforce | Assess

Smart Words

Words are defined on p. 2 of the student book. Page number of first appearance is listed below.

- **bounce**, p. 4
- **score**, p. 5
- **skill**, p. 3

Option 1: **Decoding**

 Conference

Ask students to read the Phonics Focus words on the inside back cover of *Sports Bloopers*. If they struggle with decoding, proceed to individualized instruction.

 Individualized Instruction

For words with *s*- blends: Use the Blends and Digraphs decoding routine on **page 17** to help students build accuracy.

For words with double consonants: Have students use the Word Sort decoding routine on **page 21** to sort words by their double consonant spellings.

Option 2: **Vocabulary**

 Conference

Ask students to use some Smart Words from the book in an oral sentence. Review definitions on page 2 as needed. If students demonstrate proficiency, proceed to individualized instruction.

 Individualized Instruction

The idiom *slip up* used in the first paragraph on page 3 means "to make a mistake." Build understanding of idioms by using the **Idioms** vocabulary routine on **page 25** with this expression as an example.

Option 3: **Fluency**

Conference

Ask students to read page 4 of *Sports Bloopers* aloud. To work on expressive reading, proceed to individualized instruction.

Individualized Instruction

Use pages 4–5 of *Sports Bloopers* and the **Read With Expression** fluency routine on **page 29** to have students practice expressive reading.

Comprehension

Use the questions below and the Wrap-Up on **page 35** to check comprehension and promote reader response.

After Page 4: *What happens to the basketball player who tries to stop the ball? (He slams into a table and flips over it.)*

End of Book: *Have you ever had a sports slip-up? (Answers will vary.)*

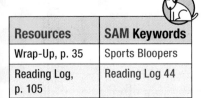

Resources	SAM Keywords
Wrap-Up, p. 35	Sports Bloopers
Reading Log, p. 105	Reading Log 44

Name _____

Sports Bloopers

Build Understanding

▶ Answer the questions below by writing details about each player's blooper. An example is done for you.

"Strike Three"
(Page 3)
Why doesn't this baseball player get a hit?

His cap slips over his face.

"Out of My Way!"
(Page 5)
What is this track star trying to do?

"Hang in There!"
(Page 5)
What slip-up does this hockey player make?

"Man Meets Wall"
(Page 6)
What happens to the ball this player was trying to catch?

"Heads Up!"
(Page 7)
How does the first soccer player get hurt?

"Bye Bye Beam!"
(Page 7)
What could be a reason this gymnast slips off the bar?

QuickWrite

▶ Which blooper title in the book do you like best? Explain why.

_____

_____

_____

BOOK 4 — Conference Guide

Fast!
by Juliette Caggiano

Genre	Pages	Lexile	Audio CD	Reading
Science	8	150	5 min 49 sec	Counts!

Summary

Some things are fast—very fast! This book features fast-growing bamboo, high-speed elevators, cheetahs that run 71 miles per hour, a speedy couch you can drive, and space probes that are the fastest vehicles in the sky.

Phonics Focus

- **Blends**

See **Master Skills Tracker:** Teacher's Guide, page 548

Skills Tracker

Preteach   Teach/Practice/Apply   Review/Reinforce   Assess

Smart Words

Words are defined on p. 2 of the student book. Page number of first appearance is listed below.

- **limit*, p. 5**
- **rate, p. 3**
- **vehicle*, p. 6**

*Spanish Cognates, **page 10**

Option 1: Decoding

 Conference

Ask students to read the Phonics Focus words on the inside back cover of *Fast!* If they struggle with decoding, proceed to individualized instruction.

Individualized Instruction

For words with blends: Use the Blends and Digraphs decoding routine on **page 17** to help students build accuracy.

Option 2: Vocabulary

Conference

Ask students to use some Smart Words listed on the inside back cover of *Fast!* in an oral sentence. Review definitions on page 2 as needed. If students demonstrate proficiency, proceed to individualized instruction.

Individualized Instruction

The idiom *check this out* used in the first paragraph of page 3 means "look at this." Build understanding of idioms using the **Idioms** vocabulary routine on **page 25** with this expression as an example.

Option 3: Fluency

 Conference

Ask students to read page 3 of *Fast!* aloud. To work on pacing, proceed to individualized instruction.

 Individualized Instruction

Use pages 3–5 of *Fast!* and the **Use Natural, Consistent Pace** fluency routine on **page 27** to have students practice reading at a natural pace.

Comprehension

Use the questions below and the Wrap-Up on **page 37** to check comprehension and promote reader response.

After Page 3: *How tall would you be if you grew as fast as bamboo?* (miles tall)

After Page 5: *What are some things that help cheetahs run fast?* (Cheetahs have long legs. Their claws grip the ground when they run.)

End of Book: *What are Helios I and Helios II?* (They are space probes, and the fastest vehicles in the sky.)

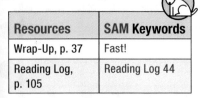

Resources	SAM Keywords
Wrap-Up, p. 37	Fast!
Reading Log, p. 105	Reading Log 44

Name _____

Fast!

Build Understanding

▶ Fill in the circles with words or phrases that tell about the cheetah.
An example is done for you.

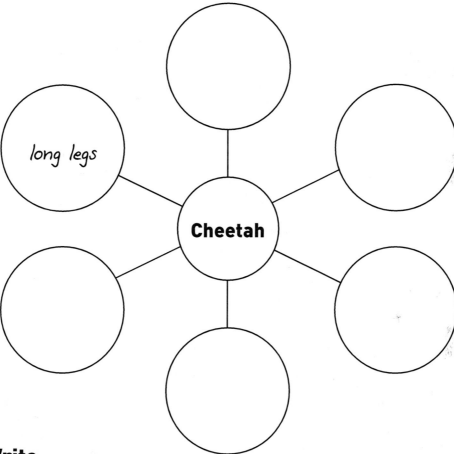

QuickWrite

▶ What other fast object or animal would you add to the book?
Explain what makes your object or animal so fast.

_____

_____

_____

Resource Links
Library Teaching Resources: p. 37
SAM Keyword: Fast!

Use with **Library Teaching Resources**, *page 36.*

System 44 Library 37

I Do Not Eat Worms (and Other Poems)

by Tina Posner

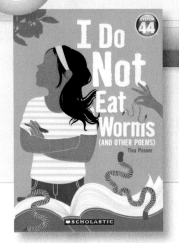

Genre	Pages	Lexile	Audio CD	Reading
Poetry	8	140	5 min 30 sec	Counts!

Summary

In this collection of poems, a girl writes about her secret journal, almost singing on TV, being her grandma's favorite, and how hard homework can be. She admits that she might not be perfect, but she certainly doesn't eat worms like her brother. The girl's poems express what's important to her, what troubles her, and what she longs for.

Phonics Focus

- Review blends
- *-ng* and *-nk*
- Double consonants

See **Master Skills Tracker:** Teacher's Guide, page 548

Skills Tracker

Preteach Teach/Practice/Apply Review/Reinforce Assess

Smart Words

Words are defined on p. 2 of the student book. Page number of first appearance is listed below.

- express*, p. 5
- journal, p. 3
- poem*, p. 3

*Spanish Cognates, **page 10**

Option 1: Decoding

 Conference

Ask students to read the Phonics Focus words on the inside back cover of *I Do Not Eat Worms*. If they struggle with decoding, proceed to individualized instruction.

 Individualized Instruction

For words with blends, and *-ng* and *-nk*: Use the Blends and Digraphs decoding routine on **page 17** to build accuracy.

For words with double consonants: Have students use the Word Sort routine on **page 21** to sort words by double consonant sounds. Supplement words as needed.

Option 2: Vocabulary

 Conference

Ask students to use some Smart Words from the book in an oral sentence. Review definitions on page 2 as needed. If students demonstrate proficiency, proceed to individualized instruction.

 Individualized Instruction

The Smart Word *express* is the base of the words *expressed, expressing, expression, expressions,* and *expressive.* Use the **Extending Meaning** vocabulary routine on **page 22** to build student familiarity with morphological word families.

Option 3: Fluency

 Conference

Ask students to read page 7 of *I Do Not Eat Worms* aloud. To work on correct phrasing, proceed to individualized instruction.

 Individualized Instruction

Use page 7 of *I Do Not Eat Worms* and the **Phrasing and Punctuation** fluency routine on **page 26** to have students practice correct phrasing.

Comprehension

Use the questions below and the Wrap-Up on **page 39** to check comprehension and promote reader response.

After Page 3: *What does the girl keep secret in the first poem?* (her journal)

After Page 6: *What nice things does the girl's grandma do for her?* (The girl's grandma cooks for her, hugs her, kisses her, and brushes her hair.)

End of Book: *What are some dreams or hopes that the girl writes about in the poems?* (She wants to sing on TV and have an easier time with her homework.)

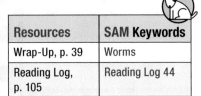

Resources	SAM Keywords
Wrap-Up, p. 39	Worms
Reading Log, p. 105	Reading Log 44

Name _____

I Do Not Eat Worms (and Other Poems)

Build Understanding

▶ In each of the poems, the girl expresses strong feelings. Write something she would think or say about each topic. The first one is done for you.

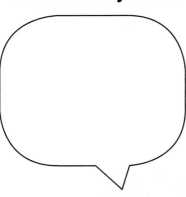

I won't tell anyone where I keep my journal because it's full of secret stuff.

1. Her secret journal

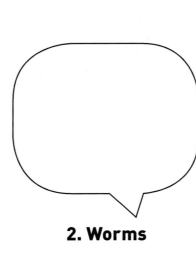

2. Worms

3. Singing on TV

4. Her Grandma

5. Homework

QuickWrite

▶ Pick one poem that best tells about your life. Write at least two sentences to explain why.

_____

_____

_____

Resource Links
Library Teaching Resources: p. 39
SAM Keyword: Worms

Use with **Library Teaching Resources,** page 38.

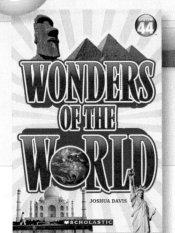

Wonders of the World

by **Joshua Davis**

Genre	Pages	Lexile	Audio CD	Reading Counts!
Social Studies	**8**	**240**	**6 min 51 sec**	

Summary

The world is full of many wonders. Some, like the Egyptian pyramids, are ancient wonders of the past. Others, like the Internet, are modern-day wonders. This book features seven well-known wonders from near and far.

Phonics Focus

- **Blends**

See **Master Skills Tracker:** Teacher's Guide, page 548

Skills Tracker

Preteach Teach/Practice/Apply Review/Reinforce Assess

Smart Words

Words are defined on p. 2 of the student book. Page number of first appearance is listed below.

- **build p. 4**
- **statue*, p. 6**
- **wonder, p. 3**

*Spanish Cognates, **page 10**

Option 1: **Decoding**

 Conference

Ask students to read the Phonics Focus words on the inside back cover of *Wonders of the World*. If they struggle with decoding, proceed to individualized instruction.

 Individualized Instruction

For words with blends: Use the Blends and Digraphs decoding routine on **page 17** to help students build accuracy.

Option 2: **Vocabulary**

Conference

Ask students to use some Smart Words listed on the inside back cover of *Wonders of the World* in an oral sentence. Review definitions on page 2 as needed. If students demonstrate proficiency, proceed to individualized instruction.

 Individualized Instruction

The Smart Word *wonder* can mean "something that is amazing or surprising" or "to be curious about something." Use the **Multiple-Meaning Words** vocabulary routine on **page 23** with *wonder* as an example to help students use context to determine the correct meaning.

Option 3: **Fluency**

 Conference

Ask students to read page 3 of *Wonders of the World* aloud. To work on pacing, proceed to individualized instruction.

 Individualized Instruction

Use pages 3–5 of *Wonders of the World* and the **Use Natural, Consistent Pace** fluency routine on **page 27** to have students practice reading at a natural pace.

Comprehension

Use the questions below and the Wrap-Up on **page 41** to check comprehension and promote reader response.

After Page 5: *How many years did it take to build the Great Wall of China? (It took more than 2,000 years.)*

End of Book: *Why did France give the Statue of Liberty to the United States? (France gave it to the United States as a hundred-year birthday present.)*

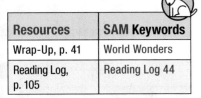

Resources	SAM Keywords
Wrap-Up, p. 41	World Wonders
Reading Log, p. 105	Reading Log 44

Name _____

Wonders of the World

Build Understanding

▶ Summarize information about each wonder below. Use the most important details from the book. An example is done for you.

Internet *(Page 3)*

The Internet connects people. People use it to find news.

They use it to send emails.

Pyramids of Giza *(Page 4)*

_____

_____

Great Wall of China *(Page 5)*

_____

_____

Statue of Liberty *(Page 7)*

_____

_____

QuickWrite

▶ What is a wonder in your life? Write two sentences to explain why.

_____

_____

Mystery Photo
by **Nancy Honovich**

Genre	Pages	Lexile	Audio CD	Reading
Science	16	240	9 min 9 sec	Counts!

Summary

This book features ten close-up mystery photos. Readers are given clues to help them identify the image in each photograph. Some of the "mysteries" include a lobster, a pizza, and rope. Answers for each mystery appear at the end of the book.

Phonics Focus

- **Closed syllables**

See **Master Skills Tracker:** Teacher's Guide, page 548

Skills Tracker

Preteach | Teach/Practice/Apply | Review/Reinforce | Assess

Smart Words

Words are defined on pp. 2–3 of the student book. Page number of first appearance is listed below.

- **guess, p. 4**
- **hint, p. 4**
- **invent*, p. 5**
- **mystery*, p. 4**
- **ordinary*, p. 4**

*Spanish Cognates, **page 10**

Option 1: **Decoding**

 Conference

Ask students to read the Phonics Focus words on the inside back cover of *Mystery Photo*. If they struggle with decoding, proceed to individualized instruction.

 Individualized Instruction

For words with closed syllables: Have students use the Syllable Strategies decoding routine on **page 16** to help students determine the correct sound for vowels in closed syllables.

Option 2: **Vocabulary**

 Conference

Ask students to use some Smart Words listed on the inside back cover of *Mystery Photo* in an oral sentence. Review definitions on pages 2–3 as needed. If students demonstrate proficiency, proceed to individualized instruction.

 Individualized Instruction

The Smart Word *invent* is the base of the words *invented, inventing, invention, inventions, inventive,* and *inventor*. Use the **Extending Meaning** vocabulary routine on **page 22** to build student familiarity with morphological word families.

Option 3: **Fluency**

 Conference

Ask students to read page 4 of *Mystery Photo* aloud. To work on correct phrasing, proceed to individualized instruction.

 Individualized Instruction

Use pages 4–5 of *Mystery Photo* and the **Phrasing and Punctuation** fluency routine on **page 26** to have students practice correct phrasing.

Comprehension

Use the questions below and the Wrap-Up on **page 43** to check comprehension and promote reader response.

After Page 7: *What countries or areas might the food on page 6 come from?* (Italy or the Middle East)

After Page 11: *Which two objects in the photos so far are made of steel?* (the Ferris wheel and the skyscraper)

End of Book: *Which people use the object pictured on page 14?* (sailors, rock climbers, and circus acrobats)

Resources	SAM Keywords
Wrap-Up, p. 43	Mystery Photo
Reading Log, p. 105	Reading Log 44

Name _____

Mystery Photo

Build Understanding

▶ Details are bits of information. Write the detail or hint that you think provides the best clue for each picture. The first one is done for you.

Topic	Details
Lightbulb *(Page 5)*	*It lights up a room.*
Pizza *(Page 6)*	
Soccer Ball *(Page 7)*	
Lobster *(Page 9)*	
Skyscraper *(Page 10)*	
Stop Sign *(Page 11)*	
Book *(Page 12)*	
Polar Bear *(Page 13)*	

QuickWrite

▶ Think of an object. Write down some clues that might help another person figure out what that object is.

_____

_____

Travels With Mapman
by Susan O'Connor

Genre	Pages	Lexile	Audio CD	Reading
Social Studies	16	240	10 min 32 sec	Counts!

Summary

Mapman takes readers on a journey to ten different sites in the United States. As readers travel through Hawaii, California, Washington, Idaho, Wyoming, Utah, Arizona, South Dakota, Pennsylvania, and New York, they learn facts about each state. They get to use their map skills, too!

Phonics Focus

- *sh*

See **Master Skills Tracker:** Teacher's Guide, page 548

Skills Tracker

Preteach | Teach/Practice/Apply | Review/Reinforce | Assess

Smart Words

Words are defined on pp. 2–3 of the student book. Page number of first appearance is listed below.

- **border**, p. 8
- **capital***, p. 6
- **coast***, p. 7
- **island***, p. 6
- **ocean***, p. 6

*Spanish Cognates, **page 11**

Option 1: **Decoding**

 Conference

Ask students to read the Phonics Focus words on the inside back cover of *Travels With Mapman*. If they struggle with decoding, proceed to individualized instruction.

 Individualized Instruction

For words with *sh*: Use the Blends and Digraphs decoding routine on **page 17** to help students build accuracy.

Option 2: **Vocabulary**

 Conference

Ask students to use some Smart Words listed on the inside back cover of *Travels With Mapman* in an oral sentence. Review definitions on pages 2–3 as needed. If students demonstrate proficiency, proceed to individualized instruction.

Individualized Instruction

The Smart Word *coast* can mean "the land that is next to a big body of water" or "to drift, float, or glide." Use the **Multiple-Meaning Words** vocabulary routine on **page 23** with *coast* as an example to help students use context to determine the correct meaning.

Option 3: **Fluency**

 Conference

Ask students to read page 6 of *Travels With Mapman* aloud. To work on correct phrasing, proceed to individualized instruction.

 Individualized Instruction

Use pages 6–7 of *Travels With Mapman* and the **Phrasing and Punctuation** fluency routine on **page 26** to have students practice correct phrasing.

Comprehension

Use the questions below and the Wrap-Up on **page 45** to check comprehension and promote reader response.

After Page 7: *What is Alcatraz and where is it?* (Alcatraz is a prison on an island near San Francisco.)

After Page 11: *What activity do people do at the Salt Flats in Utah?* (They race on land that is made of white salt.)

End of Book: *What two states should you visit if you want to see a corn palace and meet Amish people?* (South Dakota and Pennsylvania)

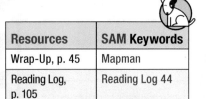

Resources	SAM **Keywords**
Wrap-Up, p. 45	Mapman
Reading Log, p. 105	Reading Log 44

Name _____

Travels With Mapman

Build Understanding

Details are bits of information. Answer the questions below with details from the book. The first one is done for you.

Hawaii *(Page 6)* What is the capital of Hawaii? *Honolulu is the capital of Hawaii.*	**Washington** *(Page 8)* What kind of boat race takes place on Green Lake in Washington?	**Idaho** *(Page 9)* What activity do people do with potatoes in Shelley, Idaho?
Utah *(Page 11)* What lake are the Salt Flats near?	**Arizona** *(Page 12)* Which river runs through Arizona?	**New York** *(Page 15)* Which city is the capital of New York?

QuickWrite

▶ Would you rather be in a milk carton race in Washington or race a car on the Salt Flats in Utah? Explain your choice. Use details from the book to support it.

_____

_____

_____

The Gift

Based on the short story "The Gift of the Magi" by O. Henry

Adapted by **Michael Leviton**

Genre	Pages	Lexile	Audio CD	Reading
Classic Retelling	**16**	**250**	**8 min 36 sec**	**Counts!**

Summary

In this retelling of "The Gift of the Magi" by O. Henry, Chet and Kendra want to celebrate their anniversary, but don't have money to buy presents. Kendra sells her guitar to buy Chet a chain for his watch. Meanwhile, Chet sells his watch to buy Kendra a guitar case. When they receive each other's gifts, they realize that love is the greatest gift of all.

Phonics Focus

- *ch, -tch*

See **Master Skills Tracker:** Teacher's Guide, page 548

Skills Tracker

Preteach | Teach/Practice/Apply | Review/Reinforce | Assess

Smart Words

Words are defined on pp. 2–3 of the student book. Page number of first appearance is listed below.

- **buy, p. 5**
- **choose, p. 6**
- **cost*, p. 7**
- **receive*, p. 7**
- **special*, p. 5**

*Spanish Cognates, **page 11**

Option 1: **Decoding**

 Conference

Ask students to read the Phonics Focus words on the inside back cover of *The Gift*. If they struggle with decoding, proceed to individualized instruction.

 Individualized Instruction

For words with *ch* and *–tch*: Use the Blends and Digraphs decoding routine on **page 17** to help students build accuracy.

Option 2: **Vocabulary**

 Conference

Ask students to use some Smart Words listed on the inside back cover of *The Gift* in an oral sentence. Review definitions on pages 2–3 as needed. If students demonstrate proficiency, proceed to individualized instruction.

 Individualized Instruction

The idiom *cheer up* used in the second paragraph of page 6 means "to make someone happier." Build understanding of idioms using the **Idioms** vocabulary routine on **page 25** with this expression as an example.

Option 3: **Fluency**

 Conference

Ask students to read page 5 of *The Gift* aloud. To work on pacing, proceed to individualized instruction.

 Individualized Instruction

Use pages 5–7 of *The Gift* and the **Use Natural, Consistent Pace** fluency routine on **page 27** to have students practice correct pacing.

Comprehension

Use the questions below and the Wrap-Up on **page 47** to check comprehension and promote reader response.

After Page 7: *Why is Kendra sad? (She wants to buy Chet a gift but she doesn't have any money.)*

After Page 11: *What does Kendra do with her guitar? (She sells it to get money to buy Chet a new watch chain.)*

End of Book: *What is the problem with the gifts that Kendra and Chet buy for each other? (They can't use the gifts because they sold the guitar and watch for money.)*

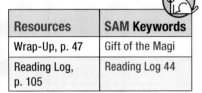

Resources	SAM Keywords
Wrap-Up, p. 47	Gift of the Magi
Reading Log, p. 105	Reading Log 44

The Gift

Build Understanding

▶ All of the events listed below are from the book, but they are out of order. Rewrite each event in the correct order. The first one is done for you.

Events
Kendra buys a watch chain.
Kendra goes to the guitar store.
Kendra sells her guitar.
Chet and Kendra open their gifts.
Chet cleans his watch.

First
Chet cleans his watch.

⬇

Second

⬇

Next

⬇

Then

⬇

Last

QuickWrite

▶ Chet and Kendra buy each other gifts they cannot use. Do you think the gifts still make them happy? Why or why not? Write a sentence that tells your opinion. Use details from the story to support your answer.

_____

_____

_____

Resource Links
Library Teaching Resources: p. 47
SAM Keyword: Gift of the Magi

Use with **Library Teaching Resources**, page 46.

Gross Bugs!
by **Kim Feltes**

Genre	Pages	Lexile	Audio CD	Reading Counts!
Science	16	190	11 min 31 sec	✓

Summary

Bugs are everywhere, both outdoors and indoors. Some live in people's beds and others live on people's bodies. Some like ticks and fleas are harmful. Others, like maggots, can actually be helpful. One thing they all share in common is that they are gross!

Phonics Focus

- **Digraph** *th*

See **Master Skills Tracker:** Teacher's Guide, page 548

Skills Tracker

Preteach | Teach/Practice/Apply | Review/Reinforce | Assess

Smart Words

Words are defined on pp. 2–3 of the student book. Page number of first appearance is listed below.

- active*, p. 6
- destroy*, p. 10
- itch, p. 6
- outdoors, p. 4
- type*, p. 8

*Spanish Cognates, **page 11**

Option 1: **Decoding**

Conference

Ask students to read the Phonics Focus words on the inside back cover of *Gross Bugs!* If they struggle with decoding, proceed to individualized instruction.

Individualized Instruction

For words with digraph *th*: Use the Blends and Digraphs decoding routine on **page 17** to help students build accuracy.

Option 2: **Vocabulary**

Conference

Ask students to use some Smart Words listed on the inside back cover of *Gross Bugs!* in an oral sentence. Review definitions on pages 2–3 as needed. If students demonstrate proficiency, proceed to individualized instruction.

Individualized Instruction

The Smart Word *type* can mean "kind or sort" or "to write using a keyboard." Use the **Multiple-Meaning Words** vocabulary routine on **page 23** with *type* as an example to help students use context to determine the correct meaning.

Option 3: **Fluency**

Conference

Ask students to read page 11 of *Gross Bugs!* aloud. To work on expressive reading, proceed to individualized instruction.

Individualized Instruction

Use pages 11–12 of *Gross Bugs!* and the **Read With Expression** fluency routine on **page 29** to have students practice expressive reading.

Comprehension

Use the questions below and the Wrap-Up on **page 49** to check comprehension and promote reader response.

After Page 5: *What do dust mites eat?* (dead skin, pet food, and people food)

After Page 10: *Which of the bugs you've read about so far can hurt people or make them sick?* (bed bugs, ticks, and centipedes)

End of Book: *What are some big problems that bugs can cause?* (Dust mites can make people sneeze; bed bugs bite; ticks, fleas, and centipedes bite and can make people sick; slugs and locusts destroy plants; stink bugs smell; and carpet beetles can ruin carpet.)

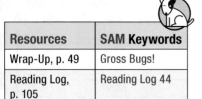

Resources	SAM Keywords
Wrap-Up, p. 49	Gross Bugs!
Reading Log, p. 105	Reading Log 44

Name _____

Gross Bugs!

Build Understanding

▶ Details are bits of information. Write two details about each gross bug. The first one is done for you.

Topic	Details
Dust Mite *(Page 5)*	• Dust mites are too small to see. • They eat dead skin.
Bed Bug *(Page 6)*	
Tick *(Page 7)*	
Cockroach *(Page 9)*	
Slug *(Page 10)*	
Maggot *(Page 12)*	
Stink Bug *(Page 14)*	
Carpet Beetle *(Page 15)*	

QuickWrite

▶ Would you want a doctor to use maggots to heal a wound on your body? Why or why not? Write two sentences to explain why.

_____

_____

Resource Links
Library Teaching Resources: p. 49
SAM Keyword: Gross Bugs!

Use with **Library Teaching Resources,** *page 48.*

Signs
by Susan O'Connor

Genre	Pages	Lexile	Audio CD	Reading
Social Studies	**16**	**200**	**8 min 9 sec**	**Counts!**

Summary

Signs are found all over the world. Some, like stop signs, look the same no matter what language they're in. Others have pictures that everyone can understand. From caution signs to animal crossing and No! signs, signs help people when they're on the go.

Phonics Focus

- *-ing* with no base change
- Review *ch, -tch, sh, th*

See **Master Skills Tracker:**
Teacher's Guide, page 548

Skills Tracker

Preteach	Teach/Practice/Apply	Review/Reinforce	Assess

Smart Words

Words are defined on pp. 2–3 of the student book. Page number of first appearance is listed below.

- allow, p. 6
- drive, p. 6
- sign, p. 4
- traffic*, p. 6
- warn, p. 6

*Spanish Cognates, **page 11**

Option 1: Decoding

 Conference

Ask students to read the Phonics Focus words on the inside back cover of *Signs*. If they struggle with decoding, proceed to individualized instruction.

 Individualized Instruction

For words with *-ing* with no base change: Use the Word Parts decoding routine on **page 18** to help students identify and use inflectional endings.

For words with *ch, -tch, sh,* and *th*: Use the Blends and Digraphs decoding routine on **page 17** to help students build accuracy.

Option 2: Vocabulary

 Conference

Ask students to use some Smart Words listed on the inside back cover of *Signs* in an oral sentence. Review definitions on pages 2–3 as needed. If students demonstrate proficiency, proceed to individualized instruction.

 Individualized Instruction

The Smart Word *sign* is the base of the words *signal, signaled, signaling, signals, signed, signing,* and *signs.* Use the **Extending Meaning** vocabulary routine on **page 22** to build student familiarity with morphological word families.

Option 3: Fluency

Conference

Ask students to read page 4 of *Signs* aloud. To work on pacing, proceed to individualized instruction.

Individualized Instruction

Use pages 4–6 of *Signs* and the **Use Natural, Consistent Pace** fluency routine on **page 27** to have students practice reading at a natural pace.

Comprehension

Use the questions below and the Wrap-Up on **page 51** to check comprehension and promote reader response.

After Page 7: *Stop signs from different countries look the same. What do they look like?* (All of the stop signs featured in the book have 8 sides and are red with white borders.)

After Page 11: *How do animal signs help animals?* (They warn people that animals are near, which helps keep animals safe.)

End of Book: *What do red lines mean when they are over a picture on a sign?* (They mean "No! Do not do this!")

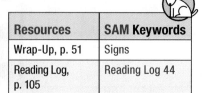

Resources	SAM Keywords
Wrap-Up, p. 51	Signs
Reading Log, p. 105	Reading Log 44

Name _____

Signs

Build Understanding

▶ Summarize the most important information about each type of sign. An example is done for you.

Stop Signs *(Pages 4–5)*

_____

_____

Traffic Signs *(Pages 6–7)*

Traffic signs tell drivers what is happening and what is allowed.

Some traffic signs warn drivers.

Caution Signs *(Pages 8–9)*

_____

_____

Animal Signs *(Pages 10–11)*

_____

_____

No! Signs *(Pages 12–13)*

_____

_____

QuickWrite

▶ Which sign do you think is easy to understand from its picture? Which is difficult to understand? Explain your answers.

_____

_____

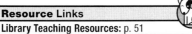

Resource Links
Library Teaching Resources: p. 51
SAM Keyword: Signs

Use with **Library Teaching Resources,** *page 50.*

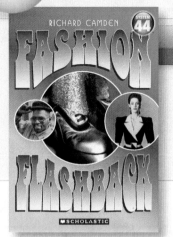

Fashion Flashback
by Richard Camden

Genre	Pages	Lexile	Audio CD	Reading
Social Studies	16	220	10 min 23 sec	Counts!

Summary

Fashion is always changing. In the 1920s, women have fun in flapper dresses, but in the 1940s, they're serious in slacks. In the 1970s people are outrageous in platforms and bellbottoms, but prefer preppie styles in the 1980s and go grunge in the 1990s. As long as people continue to enjoy wearing clothing, styles will continue to come and go.

Phonics Focus

• **-ed with no base change**

See **Master Skills Tracker:** Teacher's Guide, page 548

Skills Tracker

Preteach   Teach/Practice/Apply   Review/Reinforce   Assess

Smart Words

Words are defined on pp. 2–3 of the student book. Page number of first appearance is listed below.

• decade*, p. 9
• fashion, p. 4
• popular*, p. 4
• practical*, p. 7
• trend, p. 5

*Spanish Cognates, **page 11**

Option 1: **Decoding**

 Conference

Ask students to read the Phonics Focus words on the inside back cover of *Fashion Flashback*. If they struggle with decoding, proceed to individualized instruction.

 Individualized Instruction

For words with -ed with no base change: Have students use the Word Parts decoding routine on **page 18** to help students identify and use inflectional endings.

Option 2: **Vocabulary**

 Conference

Ask students to use some Smart Words listed on the inside back cover of *Fashion Flashback* in an oral sentence. Review definitions on pages 2–3 as needed. If students demonstrate proficiency, proceed to individualized instruction.

 Individualized Instruction

The idiom *show off* used in the second paragraph of page 9 means "to do something to get attention." Build understanding of idioms using the **Idioms** vocabulary routine on **page 25** with this expression as an example.

Option 3: **Fluency**

 Conference

Ask students to read page 10 of *Fashion Flashback* aloud. To work on correct phrasing, proceed to individualized instruction.

 Individualized Instruction

Use pages 10–11 of *Fashion Flashback* and the **Phrasing and Punctuation** fluency routine on **page 26** to have students practice correct phrasing.

Comprehension

Use the questions below and the Wrap-Up on **page 53** to check comprehension and promote reader response.

After Page 7: *What event makes women of the 1920s wear lighter, more fun dresses? (A big war ends in 1918, and women switch to lighter dresses so they can dance and have fun.)*

After Page 11: *What are some fashion trends in the 1970s? (long skirts, short skirts, suits with wide lapels, wide collars, high boots, platform shoes, bellbottom jeans, skinny jeans, sparkles, bright colors, and lots of hair)*

End of Book: *What is the look of the 1990s called? (grunge)*

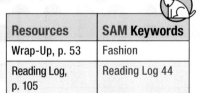

Resources	SAM Keywords
Wrap-Up, p. 53	Fashion
Reading Log, p. 105	Reading Log 44

Name _____

Fashion Flashback

Build Understanding

▶ Many styles have come and gone. Fill in the circles with some of the fashions of the past. An example is done for you.

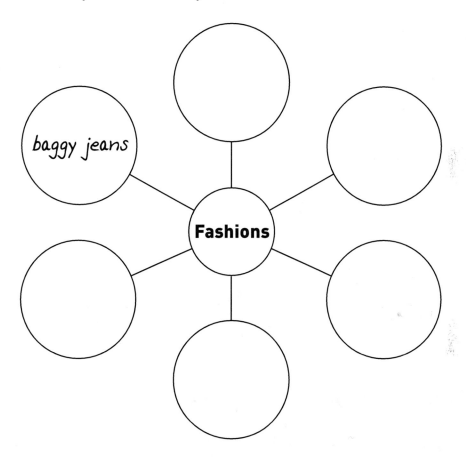

QuickWrite

▶ Which fashion from the circles above is your favorite? Describe the fashion and explain why you like it. Use details from the book to support your answer.

_____

_____

_____

Resource Links
Library Teaching Resources: p. 53
SAM Keyword: Fashion

Use with **Library Teaching Resources,** *page 52*

Button Your Lip and Other Idioms
by Polly Downes

Genre	Pages	Lexile	Audio CD	Reading Counts!
Language Arts	16	210	9 min 48 sec	

Summary

Idioms are expressions that seem to mean one thing, but really mean another. This book explains what people really mean when they say, "shake a leg," "hold your horses," "put on your thinking cap," and eight other idioms.

Phonics Focus

- **Closed syllables with schwa**

See **Master Skills Tracker:** Teacher's Guide, page 548

Skills Tracker
Preteach Teach/Practice/Apply Review/Reinforce Assess

Smart Words

Words are defined on pp. 2–3 of the student book. Page number of first appearance is listed below.

- common*, p. 4
- explain*, p. 4
- idiom, p. 4
- shake, p. 4
- tale, p. 6

*Spanish Cognates, **page 11**

Option 1: Decoding

 Conference

Ask students to read the Phonics Focus words on the inside back cover of *Button Your Lip and Other Idioms*. If they struggle with decoding, proceed to individualized instruction.

 Individualized Instruction

For words with closed syllables with schwa: Use the Syllable Strategies decoding routine on **page 16** to help students decode multisyllabic words.

Option 2: Vocabulary

 Conference

Ask students to use some Smart Words listed on the inside back cover of *Button Your Lip and Other Idioms* in an oral sentence. Review definitions on pages 2–3 as needed. If students demonstrate proficiency, proceed to individualized instruction.

 Individualized Instruction

The Smart Word *explain* is the base of the words *explained, unexplained, explaining, explains, explainable, unexplainable, explanation,* and *explanatory.* Use the **Extending Meaning** vocabulary routine on **page 22** to build student familiarity with morphological word families.

Option 3: Fluency

Conference

Ask students to read page 10 of *Button Your Lip and Other Idioms* aloud. To work on expressive reading, proceed to individualized instruction.

Individualized Instruction

Use pages 10–12 of *Button Your Lip and Other Idioms* and the **Read with Expression** fluency routine on **page 29** to have students practice expressive reading.

Comprehension

Use the questions below and the Wrap-Up on **page 55** to check comprehension and promote reader response.

After Page 6: *Where does the idiom "saved by the bell" come from?* (Hundreds of years ago, coffins had bells so that people who were buried alive could let others know.)

After Page 10: *What does the idiom "hold your horses" mean?* (Slow down and wait.)

End of Book: *Which idiom means that you've said the wrong thing at the wrong time?* (the idiom, "put your foot in your mouth")

Resources	SAM Keywords
Wrap-Up, p. 55	Button Your Lip
Reading Log, p. 105	Reading Log 44

Name _____

Button Your Lip and Other Idioms

Build Understanding

▶ Match each idiom to its meaning. The first one is done for you.

1. Backseat Driver   Hurry

2. Button Your Lip   A bossy person

3. Do Not Let the Cat Out   Think about a problem
    of the Bag

                                    Do not talk

4. Hit the Nail on the Head
                                    To be right

5. Hold Your Horses
                                    Slow down

6. Put on Your Thinking Cap
                                Say the wrong thing

7. Put Your Foot in Your Mouth   at the wrong time

8. Shake a Leg   Do not tell a secret

QuickWrite

▶ Two friends are talking, and each one uses an idiom. Write what they say to each other. Use two of the idioms above.

_____

_____

_____

Resource Links
Library Teaching Resources: p. 55
SAM Keyword: Button Your Lip

Use with **Library Teaching Resources,** *page 54.*

Conference Guide

African Journey
by Leslie Bakke and Susan O'Connor

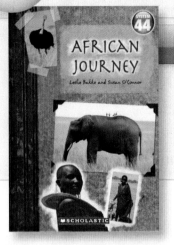

Genre	Pages	Lexile	Audio CD	Reading
Science	16	230	8 min 33 sec	Counts!

Summary

Leslie Bakke journeys to Tanzania, where she climbs Mount Kilimanjaro, the tallest mountain in Africa. She also goes on a nature safari in the Serengeti, a huge national park teeming with wildlife, and visits the Maasai, a local tribe. Her journey is recorded through a collection of vivid photos with commentary.

Phonics Focus

- **Consonant + -al, -el, or -le**

See **Master Skills Tracker:** Teacher's Guide, page 548

Skills Tracker

Preteach | Teach/Practice/Apply | Review/Reinforce | Assess

Smart Words

Words are defined on pp. 2–3 of the student book. Page number of first appearance is listed below.

- **local*, p. 7**
- **migrate*, p. 8**
- **national*, p. 5**
- **nature*, p. 4**
- **travel, p. 4**

*Spanish Cognates, **page 11**

Option 1: **Decoding**

 Conference

Ask students to read the Phonics Focus words on the inside back cover of *African Journey*. If they struggle with decoding, proceed to individualized instruction.

 Individualized Instruction

For words with consonants + -al, -el, or -le: Use the Syllable Strategies decoding routine on **page 16** to help students determine the correct vowel sounds for -al, -el, and -le.

Option 2: **Vocabulary**

 Conference

Ask students to use some Smart Words listed on the inside back cover of *African Journey* in an oral sentence. Review definitions on pages 2–3 as needed. If students demonstrate proficiency, proceed to individualized instruction.

 Individualized Instruction

Use the **Context Clues** vocabulary routine on **page 24** with the Smart Word *migrate* to help students use context clues to determine meaning.

Option 3: **Fluency**

 Conference

Ask students to read page 8 of *African Journey* aloud. To work on correct phrasing, proceed to individualized instruction.

 Individualized Instruction

Use pages 8–11 of *African Journey* and the **Phrasing and Punctuation** fluency routine on **page 26** to have students practice correct phrasing.

Comprehension

Use the questions below and the Wrap-Up on **page 57** to check comprehension and promote reader response.

After Page 7: *How long does it take Leslie to climb Mount Kilimanjaro? (one week)*

After Page 10: *The zebras look like they're hugging, but they are not. What are they doing? (They are resting and helping each other by looking out for lions.)*

End of Book: *What is the name of the tribe that Leslie visits and what do they raise? (The tribe is called the Maasai. They raise cattle.)*

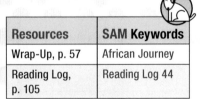

Resources	SAM Keywords
Wrap-Up, p. 57	African Journey
Reading Log, p. 105	Reading Log 44

Name _____

African Journey

▶ Build Understanding

Details are bits of information. Write two details about each topic from the book. The first one is done for you.

Topic	Details
Mount Kilimanjaro *(Pages 6–7)*	• *Mount Kilimanjaro is the tallest mountain in Africa.* • *There is a glacier at the top of the mountain.*
Going on Safari *(Pages 8–9)*	
Animal Buddies *(Pages 10–11)*	
On the Hunt *(Pages 12–13)*	
Visiting the Maasai *(Pages 14–15)*	

QuickWrite

▶ If you could travel anywhere in the world, where would you go? What would you want to see there? Use at least one detail to support your answer.

_____

_____

_____

Resource Links
Library Teaching Resources: p. 57
SAM Keyword: African Journey

*Use with **Library Teaching Resources**, page 56.*

Ripped From the Headlines
by **Peter Gutiérrez**

BOOK 15   Conference Guide

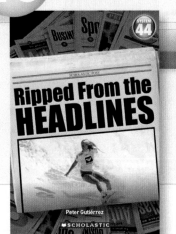

Genre	Pages	Lexile	Audio CD	Reading
Social Studies	**16**	**210**	**10 min 28 sec**	**Counts!**

Summary

Wild stories make the headlines. Bethany makes the news after a shark bites off her arm. Felix catches a baby thrown out the window of a burning building. A hiker named Aron cuts off his own arm to save his life. These stories and others are featured in this book about brave heroes and amazing circumstances.

Phonics Focus

- **Long *a* with final *e***
- **Long *i* with final *e***

See **Master Skills Tracker:** Teacher's Guide, page 548

Skills Tracker

Preteach | Teach/Practice/Apply | Review/Reinforce | Assess

Smart Words

Words are defined on pp. 2–3 of the student book. Page number of first appearance is listed below.

- **amaze**, p. 4
- **believe**, p. 4
- **brave**, p. 4
- **danger**, p. 5
- **rescue***, p. 6

*Spanish Cognates, **page 11**

Option 1: **Decoding**

 Conference

Ask students to read the Phonics Focus words on the inside back cover of *Ripped From the Headlines*. If they struggle with decoding, proceed to individualized instruction.

 Individualized Instruction

For words with long *a* and *i* with final *e*: Have students use the Word Sort decoding routine on **page 21** to sort words by long vowel sound. Point out that a final *e* can control a long vowel sound to make it long.

Option 2: **Vocabulary**

 Conference

Ask students to use some Smart Words listed on the inside back cover of *Ripped From the Headlines* in an oral sentence. Review definitions on pages 2–3 as needed. If students demonstrate proficiency, proceed to individualized instruction.

 Individualized Instruction

The Smart Word *brave* can mean "not afraid" or "to do something unpleasant and difficult," as in "He braved the storm." Use the **Multiple-Meaning Words** vocabulary routine on **page 23** with *brave* as an example to help students use context to determine the correct meaning.

Option 3: **Fluency**

 Conference

Ask students to read page 12 of *Ripped from the Headlines* aloud. To work on pacing, proceed to individualized instruction.

 Individualized Instruction

Use pages 12–13 of *Ripped From the Headlines* and the **Use Natural, Consistent Pace** fluency routine on **page 27** to have students practice reading at a natural pace.

Comprehension

Use the questions below and the Wrap-Up on **page 59** to check comprehension and promote reader response.

After Page 7: *What happens to Muhammet? (He survives after being trapped for five days under the rubble of a building.)*

After Page 9: *What happens to Palmira and who saves her? (A strange man grabs her while her gym class is outside in a park. Her friends attack the man and save her.)*

End of Book: *How does Aron's brave act save his life? (Cutting off his own arm allows him to get out from under the rock and find help.)*

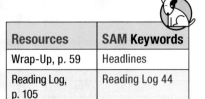

Resources	SAM Keywords
Wrap-Up, p. 59	Headlines
Reading Log, p. 105	Reading Log 44

Name _____

Ripped From the Headlines

Build Understanding

▶ Summarize each story below in your own words. One has been done for you as an example.

"Shark Attack!" *(Page 5)*

Bethany is surfing when a shark bites off her arm. A friend helps save Bethany's life. Today, Bethany is still surfing.

"Stranger Danger!" *(Pages 8–9)*

_____

_____

"Falling Baby!" *(Pages 12–13)*

_____

_____

"Trapped!" *(Pages 14-15)*

_____

_____

QuickWrite

▶ If you were Bethany or Aron, would you want to go surfing or hiking again after what happened to you? Why or why not? Explain your answer.

_____

_____

Win or Lose?

by **Sunita Apte**

Genre	Pages	Lexile	Audio CD	Reading
Fiction	16	210	8 min 37 sec	Counts!

Summary

Dan isn't very good at soccer, but he joins the soccer team anyway. Ray, the team's ace player, is upset because Dan could cost the team first place. Grace is the only team member who wants to give Dan a chance. When Ray messes up during the next game and Dan makes a good pass, Ray realizes he shouldn't have judged Dan so harshly.

Phonics Focus

- Soft *c* and *g*
- Suffixes *–ment* and *–ness*

See **Master Skills Tracker:** Teacher's Guide, page 548

Skills Tracker

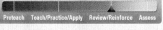

Preteach Teach/Practice/Apply Review/Reinforce Assess

Smart Words

Words are defined on pp. 2–3 of the student book. Page number of first appearance is listed below.

- coach, p. 9
- important*, p. 6
- kick, p. 4
- practice*, p. 4
- team, p. 4

*Spanish Cognates, **page 11**

Option 1: Decoding

 Conference

Ask students to read the Phonics Focus words on the inside back cover of *Win or Lose?* If they struggle with decoding, proceed to individualized instruction.

 Individualized Instruction

For words with soft *c* and *g*: Have students use the Word Sort decoding routine on **page 21** to sort by soft *c* and *g* sounds.

For words with suffixes *-ment* and *-ness*: Use the Word Parts decoding routine on **page 18** to help students identify and use suffixes.

Option 2: Vocabulary

 Conference

Ask students to use some Smart Words from the book in an oral sentence. Review definitions on pages 2–3 as needed. If students demonstrate proficiency, proceed to individualized instruction.

 Individualized Instruction

The idiom *messed up* used in the first paragraph of page 13 means "made a mistake." Build understanding of idioms using the **Idioms** vocabulary routine on **page 25** with this expression as an example.

Option 3: Fluency

 Conference

Ask students to read page 12 of *Win or Lose?* aloud. To work on expressive reading, proceed to individualized instruction.

 Individualized Instruction

Use pages 12–13 of *Win or Lose?* and the **Read With Expression** fluency routine on **page 29** to have students practice expressive reading.

Comprehension

Use the questions below and the Wrap-Up on **page 61** to check comprehension and promote reader response.

After Page 7: *How do Ray and Grace feel about Dan? (Ray is upset and doesn't want him on the team. Grace welcomes him and wants to give him a chance.)*

After Page 11: *Why is Grace sad? (She's sad because everyone is mad at her for sticking up for Dan and because soccer is no longer fun.)*

End of Book: *When does Ray realize that he shouldn't have judged Dan so harshly? (He realizes this when he messes up and Grace asks him how he'd feel if the team didn't want him to play anymore.)*

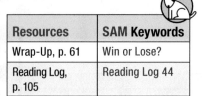

Resources	SAM Keywords
Wrap-Up, p. 61	Win or Lose?
Reading Log, p. 105	Reading Log 44

Name _____

Win or Lose?

Build Understanding

▶ Dan has just joined the team. But he may not feel wanted. Fill in the bubbles below. Write a sentence that tells what each person might be thinking. An example is done for you.

The rules are that everyone gets to play.

Coach

Ray

Dan

Grace

QuickWrite

▶ Why does Ray finally give Dan a chance? Explain your answer. Use details from the book.

_____

_____

_____

Resource Links
Library Teaching Resources: p. 61
SAM Keyword: Win or Lose?

Use with **Library Teaching Resources,** *page 60.*

System 44 Library **61**

Cool Jobs in Basketball
by Peter Gutiérrez

Genre	Pages	Lexile	Audio CD	Reading
Jobs	16	300	9 min 51 sec	Counts!

Summary

Jobs in professional basketball aren't only for athletes. Yvonne Nelson is an intern who plans events for basketball teams. Tony Mejia is a reporter who writes about basketball. Keith Jones helps injured athletes and makes important team decisions. These individuals have found ways to use their skills and be part of basketball.

Phonics Focus

- Words with VC*e*
- Prefixes *non-* and *un-*

See **Master Skills Tracker:** Teacher's Guide, page 548

Skills Tracker

Preteach   Teach/Practice/Apply   Review/Reinforce   Assess

Smart Words

Words are defined on pp. 4–5 of the student book. Page number of first appearance is listed below.

- athlete*, p. 6
- business, p. 6
- experience*, p. 7
- hire, p. 6
- intern*, p. 8
- rely, p. 9

*Spanish Cognates, **page 12**

Option 1: Decoding

 Conference

Ask students to read the Phonics Focus words on the inside back cover of *Cool Jobs in Basketball*. If they struggle with decoding, proceed to individualized instruction.

 Individualized Instruction

For words with VC*e*: Have students use the Word Sort decoding routine on **page 21** to sort by long *i*, *o*, and *u* sounds.

For words with prefixes *non-* and *un-*: Use the Word Parts decoding routine on **page 18** to help students identify and use prefixes.

Option 2: Vocabulary

 Conference

Ask students to use some Smart Words from the book in an oral sentence. Review definitions on pages 4–5 as needed. If students demonstrate proficiency, proceed to individualized instruction.

 Individualized Instruction

The Smart Word *rely* has many possible synonyms and antonyms. Use the **Extending Meaning** vocabulary routine on **page 22** to extend meaning.

Option 3: Fluency

 Conference

Ask students to read page 8 of *Cool Jobs in Basketball* aloud. To work on correct phrasing, proceed to individualized instruction.

 Individualized Instruction

Use pages 8–9 of *Cool Jobs in Basketball* and the **Phrasing and Punctuation** fluency routine on **page 26** to have students practice correct phrasing.

Comprehension

Use the questions below and the Wrap-Up on **page 63** to check comprehension and promote reader response.

After Chapter 1: *Why isn't professional basketball only for athletes? (There are jobs in professional basketball for people with all kinds of experience.)*

After Chapter 3: *What jobs do Yvonne and Tony have? (Yvonne is an intern who promotes the teams and plans events. Tony writes about basketball for a Web site.)*

End of Book: *How does Keith help the players he works with? (Keith helps injured athletes by teaching them exercises to make them better.)*

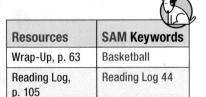

Resources	SAM Keywords
Wrap-Up, p. 63	Basketball
Reading Log, p. 105	Reading Log 44

Name _____

Cool Jobs in Basketball

Build Understanding

▶ How might Yvonne, Tony, and Keith describe their jobs? In the speech bubbles below, write what they might say. The first one is done for you.

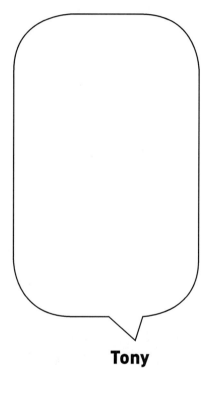

I'm an intern. I make sure the athletes look good for ads. I also plan events. I love all the friends I've made.

Yvonne

Tony

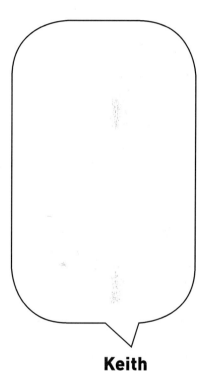

Keith

QuickWrite

▶ Which job do you think you would like most? Why? Support your answer with information from the book.

_____

_____

_____

Resource Links
Library Teaching Resources: p. 63
SAM Keyword: Basketball

Use with **Library Teaching Resources,** *page 62.*

Meet the Dragon Slayers
by **Julia Campbell**

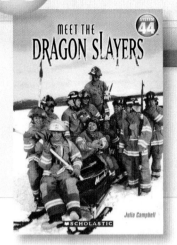

Genre	Pages	Lexile	Audio CD	Reading
Social Studies	**16**	**330**	**10 min 12 sec**	**Counts!**

Summary

Aniak, Alaska, is a geographically isolated town that needs a system to handle emergencies. The town's fire chief responds by forming the Dragon Slayers, a rescue crew of teen volunteers, to help in emergency situations. To become a Dragon Slayer, teens complete intensive training that prepares them to handle fires and medical emergencies. When emergencies happen, their expertise saves lives.

Phonics Focus

- Ending -*ing*
- Ending -*ing* with base change

See **Master Skills Tracker:** Teacher's Guide, page 548

Skills Tracker

Preteach | Teach/Practice/Apply | Review/Reinforce | Assess

Smart Words

Words are defined on pp. 4–5 of the student book. Page number of first appearance is listed below.

- **accident*, p. 6**
- **crew, p. 8**
- **emergency*, p. 6**
- **respond*, p. 6**
- **training*, p. 9**
- **volunteer*, p. 6**

*Spanish Cognates, **page 12**

Option 1: **Decoding**

 Conference

Ask students to read the Phonics Focus words on the inside back cover of *Meet the Dragon Slayers*. If they struggle with decoding, proceed to individualized instruction.

 Individualized Instruction

For words with ending -*ing* with and without base change: Use the Word Parts decoding routine on **page 18** to help students identify and use inflectional endings.

Option 2: **Vocabulary**

 Conference

Ask students to use some Smart Words listed on the inside back cover of *Meet the Dragon Slayers* in an oral sentence. Review definitions on pages 4–5 as needed. If students demonstrate proficiency, proceed to individualized instruction.

 Individualized Instruction

The idiom *pays off* used in the last paragraph of page 11 means "results in success." Build understanding of idioms using the **Idioms** vocabulary routine on **page 25** with this expression as an example.

Option 3: **Fluency**

 Conference

Ask students to read page 9 of *Meet the Dragon Slayers* aloud. To work on pacing, proceed to individualized instruction.

 Individualized Instruction

Use pages 9–11 of *Meet the Dragon Slayers* and the **Use Natural, Consistent Pace** fluency routine on **page 27** to have students practice correct pacing.

Comprehension

Use the questions below and the Wrap-Up on **page 65** to check comprehension and promote reader response.

After Chapter 1: *Why does the town of Aniak need a rescue team?* (Aniak is isolated. In emergencies, people have to wait a long time for help to come.)

After Chapter 3: *What happens to the boy who gets in a snowmobile accident? How do the Slayers help?* (He hits a truck and breaks his jaw, skull, and neck. The Slayers stop his bleeding and stay with him until a plane arrives.)

End of Book: *Why is the job of a Dragon Slayer important?* (The Dragon Slayers help people and save lives in emergency situations.)

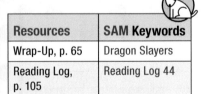

Resources	SAM Keywords
Wrap-Up, p. 65	Dragon Slayers
Reading Log, p. 105	Reading Log 44

Name _____

Meet the Dragon Slayers

Build Understanding

▶ Fill in the solution to each problem listed below. One has been done for you.

Problem	Solution
1. Emergency help takes too long to arrive in Aniak. *(Chapter 1)*	
2. Fire Chief Brown doesn't have money to pay a rescue crew. *(Chapter 1)*	
3. During an emergency, Slayers may find that a person's heart or breathing has stopped. *(Chapter 2)*	*The Slayers try CPR. This is a way to start someone's heart or help a person breathe.*
4. A boy gets seriously hurt when he hits a truck that is hidden in the snow. *(Chapter 3)*	
5. The boy needs help but there is a big snowstorm. *(Chapter 3)*	

QuickWrite

▶ The Dragon Slayers train to help others. Their training also helps them. Tell how. Use examples from the book.

_____

_____

Resource Links
Library Teaching Resources: p. 65
SAM Keyword: Dragon Slayers

Use with **Library Teaching Resources,** page 64.

Crash!
by Steph Smith

Genre	Pages	Lexile	Audio CD	Reading
Science	16	320	10 min 12 sec	Counts!

Summary

Scientists are keeping track of asteroids, especially one named Apophis. Experts tracking Apophis know that in the future it will fly by Earth. If Apophis crashes into Earth, it will create tremendous damage. Scientists have some ideas about how to knock an asteroid off its path. They just hope it won't get too close!

Phonics Focus

- -ed with no base change
- -ed with base change
- y as a vowel

See **Master Skills Tracker:** Teacher's Guide, page 548

Skills Tracker

Preteach | Teach/Practice/Apply | Review/Reinforce | Assess

Smart Words

Words are defined on pp. 4–5 of the student book. Page number of first appearance is listed below.

- expert*, p. 7
- follow, p. 7
- gravity*, p. 12
- orbit*, p. 10
- telescope*, p. 10

*Spanish Cognates, **page 12**

Option 1: Decoding

 Conference

Ask students to read the Phonics Focus words on the inside back cover of *Crash!* If they struggle with decoding, proceed to individualized instruction.

 Individualized Instruction

For words with -ed with and without base change: Use the Word Parts decoding routine on **page 18** to help students identify and use inflectional endings.

For words with y as a vowel: Have students use the Word Sort decoding routine on **page 21** to sort words by long e, long i, and short i sounds.

Option 2: Vocabulary

 Conference

Ask students to use some Smart Words from the book in an oral sentence. Review definitions on pages 4–5 as needed. If students demonstrate proficiency, proceed to individualized instruction.

 Individualized Instruction

The Smart Word *follow* can mean "to watch or keep track of something as it moves" or "to chase or pursue." Use the **Multiple-Meaning Words** vocabulary routine on **page 23** with *follow* as an example to help students determine the correct meaning.

Option 3: Fluency

 Conference

Ask students to read page 10 of *Crash!* aloud. To work on expressive reading, proceed to individualized instruction.

 Individualized Instruction

Use pages 10–11 of *Crash!* and the **Read With Expression** fluency routine on **page 29** to have students practice expressive reading.

Comprehension

Use the questions below and the Wrap-Up on **page 67** to check comprehension and promote reader response.

After Chapter 1: *What is an asteroid? (It is a big rock that flies around in space.)*

After Chapter 2: *What ideas do experts have about how to stop an asteroid from hitting Earth? (The asteroid can be pushed away by a spaceship that crashes into it. Or, it can be pulled away using the force of gravity from a big ship.)*

End of Book: *When Apophis flies by Earth again in 2029, where will be the best place to see it? (The best place to see it will be in Europe.)*

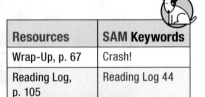

Resources	SAM Keywords
Wrap-Up, p. 67	Crash!
Reading Log, p. 105	Reading Log 44

Name _____

Crash!

Build Understanding

▶ Identify the most important ideas in each chapter. Then, summarize the chapter in your own words. One has been done for you as an example.

Chapter 1: "Look! An Asteroid!"

_____

_____

_____

Chapter 2: "On the Right Track"

An asteroid named Apophis could hit Earth. Scientists are studying it and tracking it. Experts have ideas about how to throw an asteroid off track to prevent it from slamming into Earth.

Chapter 3: "Out of This World"

_____

_____

_____

QuickWrite

▶ Should people be worried about Apophis hitting Earth? Tell why or why not. Use details from the book.

_____

_____

_____

Resource Links
Library Teaching Resources: p. 67
SAM Keyword: Crash!

Use with **Library Teaching Resources**, page 66.

The Champ and Other Stories
by **Michael Leviton**

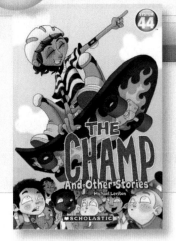

Genre	Pages	Lexile	Audio CD	Reading
Classic Retelling	**16**	**270**	**10 min 58 sec**	**Counts!**

Summary

Three updated Aesop's fables teach some classic lessons. In "The Champ," Ricky winds up in a mud puddle and learns to look before he leaps. In "The Bucket of Money," Kelly finds money, but realizes she shouldn't count her chickens before they've hatched. Finally, in "The Bugs," Andy thinks it's fun to cry wolf until he really needs help and his brother won't listen.

Phonics Focus

- **Suffixes –y and –ly**
- **Change y to i**

See **Master Skills Tracker:** Teacher's Guide, page 548

Skills Tracker

Preteach Teach/Practice/Apply Review/Reinforce Assess

Smart Words

Words are defined on pp. 4–5 of the student book. Page number of first appearance is listed below.

- **boring, p. 14**
- **challenge, p. 7**
- **contest, p. 7**
- **enjoy, p. 7**
- **instant*, p. 7**
- **trick, p. 8**

*Spanish Cognates, **page 12**

Option 1: **Decoding**

Conference

Ask students to read the Phonics Focus words on the inside back cover of *The Champ and Other Stories*. If they struggle with decoding, proceed to individualized instruction.

Individualized Instruction

For words with suffixes –y and –ly and words in which y changes to i: Use the Word Parts decoding routine on **page 18** to help students identify and use suffixes and inflectional endings.

Option 2: **Vocabulary**

Conference

Ask students to use some Smart Words listed on the inside back cover of *The Champ and Other Stories* in an oral sentence. Review definitions on pages 4–5 as needed. If students demonstrate proficiency, proceed to individualized instruction.

Individualized Instruction

The Smart Word *trick* can mean "a stunt or skillful move" or "to fool or cheat someone." Use the **Multiple-Meaning Words** vocabulary routine on **page 23** with *trick* as an example to help students use context to determine the correct meaning.

Option 3: **Fluency**

Conference

Ask students to read page 10 of *The Champ and Other Stories* aloud. To work on correct phrasing, proceed to individualized instruction.

Individualized Instruction

Use pages 10–11 of *The Champ and Other Stories* and the **Phrasing and Punctuation** fluency routine on **page 26** to have students practice correct phrasing.

Comprehension

Use the questions below and the Wrap-Up on **page 69** to check comprehension and promote reader response.

After Page 8: *What does Carlos challenge Ricky to do? (shut his eyes, spin ten times, and jump)*

After Page 12: *How does Kelly lose her money? (She trips in the street and the money rolls down a drain.)*

End of Book: *Why doesn't Chad help when bugs are crawling on Andy? (He thinks Andy is playing another trick on him.)*

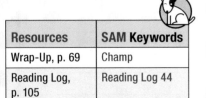

Resources	SAM Keywords
Wrap-Up, p. 69	Champ
Reading Log, p. 105	Reading Log 44

Name _____

The Champ and Other Stories

Build Understanding

▶ Suppose that Ricky, Kelly, and Andy want to tell each other the lessons they learned. What would they say? Fill in the speech bubbles below. An example is done for you.

The lesson I learned is to look before I leap.

Ricky   **Kelly**   **Andy**

QuickWrite

▶ Why does Ricky listen to Carlos even though he knows he shouldn't? Write a sentence that tells your opinion. Support your answer with details from the book.

_____

_____

_____

Resource Links
Library Teaching Resources: p. 69
SAM Keyword: Champ

Use with **Library Teaching Resources,** *page 68.*

From the Heart
by **Meredith Phillips**

Genre	Pages	Lexile	Audio CD	Reading
Science	16	280	9 min 46 sec	Counts!

Summary

Seven-year-old Adrian needs a new heart. Adrian's parents bring him to a Texas hospital for a heart transplant, but the surgery is expensive. Many kind people raise money for Adrian's surgery. Then, his doctors wait for an available heart. When a match is found, the surgery begins. It is a success, and Adrian will likely make a full recovery.

Phonics Focus

- Silent letters
- *ph*
- Digraph *wh-*
- Review inflectional endings *-ed, -ing*

See **Master Skills Tracker:** Teacher's Guide, page 548

Skills Tracker

Preteach Teach/Practice/Apply Review/Reinforce Assess

Smart Words

Words are defined on pp. 4–5 of the student book. Page number of first appearance is listed below.

- donate*, p. 8
- infection*, p. 6
- reject, p. 10
- severe, p. 8
- surgery*, p. 8
- survive*, p. 10

*Spanish Cognates, **page 12**

Resources	SAM Keywords
Wrap-Up, p. 71	From the Heart
Reading Log, p. 105	Reading Log 44

Option 1: **Decoding**

 Conference

Ask students to read the Phonics Focus words on the inside back cover of *From the Heart*. If they struggle with decoding, proceed to individualized instruction.

Individualized Instruction

For words with digraph *wh-*: Use the Blends and Digraphs decoding routine on **page 17** to help students build accuracy.

For words with *-ed* and *-ing*: Use the Word Parts decoding routine on **page 18** to help students identify and use inflectional endings.

Option 2: **Vocabulary**

 Conference

Ask students to use some Smart Words from the book in an oral sentence. Review definitions on pages 4–5 as needed. If students demonstrate proficiency, proceed to individualized instruction.

 Individualized Instruction

Use the **Context Clues** vocabulary routine on **page 24** with the Smart Word *donate* to help students use context clues to determine meaning.

Option 3: **Fluency**

 Conference

Ask students to read page 6 of *From the Heart* aloud. To work on pacing, proceed to individualized instruction.

 Individualized Instruction

Use pages 6–8 of *From the Heart* and the **Use Natural, Consistent Pace** fluency routine on **page 27** to have students practice reading with a natural pace.

Comprehension

Use the questions below and the Wrap-Up on **page 71** to check comprehension and promote reader response.

After Chapter 1: *What kind of surgery does Adrian need? (He needs a heart transplant.)*

After Chapter 3: *Where does Adrian's new heart come from? (It comes from the body of someone who has just died.)*

End of Book: *What do the doctors still worry about? (They worry that Adrian will get another infection, or that his body will reject the heart.)*

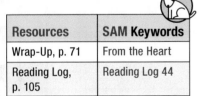

Name ____________________

From the Heart

Build Understanding

▶ Identify the most important details from the story and summarize each chapter in the spaces provided. The first one has been done for you.

Chapter 1: "A Hurting Heart"

Adrian has a rare infection. He needs a heart transplant. People donate money for the operation.

Chapter 2: "Hope and Worry"

____

____

Chapter 3: "Adrian's Surgery"

____

____

Chapter 4: "A New Chance"

____

____

QuickWrite

▶ Write at least one sentence that explains why "Hope and Worry" is a good title for the second chapter. Use details from the book to support your answer.

____

____

____

Resource Links
Library Teaching Resources: p. 71
SAM Keyword: From the Heart

Use with **Library Teaching Resources,** *page 70.*

BOOK 22 Conference Guide

The Mummy King
by **Sean McCollum**

Genre	Pages	Lexile		Audio CD		Reading
Social Studies	**16**	**250**		**10 min 10 sec**		**Counts!**

Summary

Tut is a boy when he becomes the king of ancient Egypt, and only 18 when he dies. After his death, Tut is mummified and placed in an underground tomb with treasures to be used in the afterlife. In the 1920s, Howard Carter and his team uncover Tut's tomb. The richness of their find makes both Carter and King Tut famous.

Phonics Focus

- **Open syllables**
- **Unstressed open syllables**

See **Master Skills Tracker:** Teacher's Guide, page 548

Skills Tracker

Preteach Teach/Practice/Apply Review/Reinforce Assess

Smart Words

Words are defined on pp. 4–5 of the student book. Page number of first appearance is listed below.

- **kingdom, p. 7**
- **magnificent*, p. 7**
- **mummy*, p. 8**
- **rule, p. 7**
- **temple*, p. 6**
- **tomb*, p. 11**

*Spanish Cognates, **page 12**

Option 1: **Decoding**

 Conference

Ask students to read the Phonics Focus words on the inside back cover of *The Mummy King*. If they struggle with decoding, proceed to individualized instruction.

 Individualized Instruction

For words with open syllables and unstressed open syllables: Use the Syllable Strategies routine on **page 16** to help students determine the correct vowel sounds in open syllables.

Option 2: **Vocabulary**

 Conference

Ask students to use some Smart Words listed on the inside back cover of *The Mummy King* in an oral sentence. Review definitions on pages 4–5 as needed. If students demonstrate proficiency, proceed to individualized instruction.

 Individualized Instruction

The Smart Word *rule* can mean "to have power over something" or "a law." Use the **Multiple-Meaning Words** vocabulary routine on **page 23** with *rule* as an example to help students use context to determine the correct meaning.

Option 3: **Fluency**

 Conference

Ask students to read page 8 of *The Mummy King* aloud. To work on correct phrasing, proceed to individualized instruction.

 Individualized Instruction

Use pages 8–9 of *The Mummy King* and the **Phrasing and Punctuation** fluency routine on **page 26** to have students practice correct phrasing.

Comprehension

Use the questions below and the Wrap-Up on **page 73** to check comprehension and promote reader response.

After Chapter 1: *What happens to King Tut when he dies? (His body is made into a mummy.)*

After Chapter 2: *How does Carter finally find King Tut's tomb? (A boy on Carter's team finds it when his foot hits a step.)*

End of Book: *What does Carter discover in King Tut's tomb? (magnificent jewelry, thrones, Tut's organs, a gold coffin, and Tut's mummy)*

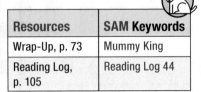

Resources	SAM **Keywords**
Wrap-Up, p. 73	Mummy King
Reading Log, p. 105	Reading Log 44

Name _____

The Mummy King

Build Understanding

▶ Answer the questions below by writing details from the book. An example has been done for you.

Chapter 1

Why does King Tut need help to rule Egypt?

He is only a young boy and doesn't know how to rule or deal with other kings.

What do the people of ancient Egypt believe will happen to King Tut after he dies?

Chapter 2

What is Howard Carter's Job?

What does he finally discover after a six-year search?

Chapter 3

What does Carter find inside the big stone box?

How many coffins surround King Tut's mummy?

QuickWrite

▶ You are Howard Carter. Yesterday, you found King Tut's tomb. Write a short letter to a friend back home. Use at least one detail from above to tell your friend what happened.

_____

_____

_____

BOOK 23 Conference Guide

Disaster!
by **Sean Price**

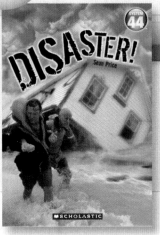

Genre	Pages	Lexile	Audio CD	Reading
Science	24	330	13 min 35 sec	Counts!

Summary

When tornadoes, tsunamis, and hurricanes strike, the result is often disaster. In 1999, tornadoes roar through Oklahoma and other states. In 2004, a tsunami in the Indian Ocean kills over 280,000 people. In 2005, Hurricane Katrina causes the New Orleans levees to break, flooding the city. Read how survivors of these disasters rebuild their homes and their lives.

Phonics Focus

• *com-* and *con-*

See **Master Skills Tracker:** Teacher's Guide, page 548

Skills Tracker

Preteach   Teach/Practice/Apply   Review/Reinforce   Assess

Smart Words

Words are defined on pp. 4–5 of the student book. Page number of first appearance is listed below.

• **aid, p. 16**
• **damage, p. 6**
• **escape*, p. 14**
• **massive*, p. 12**
• **survivor, p. 16**
• **warning, p. 10**

*Spanish Cognates, **page 13**

Option 1: **Decoding**

 Conference

Ask students to read the Phonics Focus words on the inside back cover of *Disaster!* If they struggle with decoding, proceed to individualized instruction.

Individualized Instruction

For words with *com-* and *con-* : Use the Word Parts decoding routine on **page 18** to help students identify and use prefixes.

Option 2: **Vocabulary**

 Conference

Ask students to use some Smart Words listed on the inside back cover of *Disaster!* in an oral sentence. Review definitions on pages 4–5 as needed. If students demonstrate proficiency, proceed to individualized instruction.

 Individualized Instruction

The Smart Word *aid* has many possible synonyms and antonyms. Use the **Extending Meaning** vocabulary routine on **page 22** to extend meaning.

Option 3: **Fluency**

 Conference

Ask students to read page 6 of *Disaster!* aloud. To work on pacing, proceed to individualized instruction.

 Individualized Instruction

Use pages 6–8 of *Disaster!* and the **Use Natural, Consistent Pace** fluency routine on **page 27** to have students practice correct pacing.

Comprehension

Use the questions below and the Wrap-Up on **page 75** to check comprehension and promote reader response.

After Chapter 1: *What happens to Kaci's home during the tornado? (The power goes out, the outer walls shake apart, and then the roof flies off.)*

After Chapter 2: *What kind of damage does the 2004 tsunami cause? (It kills at least 280,000 people and leaves survivors homeless.)*

End of Book: *What happens to the levees in New Orleans? (They break and water pours in, flooding most of New Orleans.)*

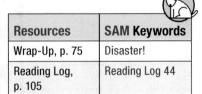

Resources	SAM Keywords
Wrap-Up, p. 75	Disaster!
Reading Log, p. 105	Reading Log 44

Name _____

Disaster!

Build Understanding

▶ Kaci, Fitri, and Troy all survive disasters. Imagine that they can all speak to each other. What would they tell each other about their experiences? Write what they would say.

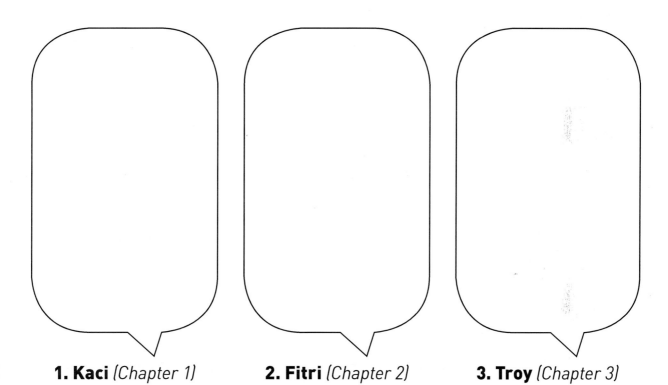

1. Kaci *(Chapter 1)*   **2. Fitri** *(Chapter 2)*   **3. Troy** *(Chapter 3)*

QuickWrite

▶ After the tsunami hits, many people help Fitri and other victims. What do you think you could do to help a victim of a natural disaster? Write some ideas below.

_____

_____

_____

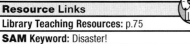

Resource Links
Library Teaching Resources: p.75
SAM Keyword: Disaster!

Use with **Library Teaching Resources,** *page 74.*

In Search of the Giant Squid
by **Britt Norlander**

Genre	Pages	Lexile	Audio CD	Reading
Science	24	350	13 min 29 sec	Counts!

Summary

Tales from Norwegian sailors tell of an elusive giant sea creature called the Kraken. When a giant sea creature washes ashore, scientists say that the Kraken is actually a giant squid. The giant squid proves difficult to find. But, in 2005, Japanese scientists find and photograph one before it gets away. Scientists still hope to capture one alive.

Phonics Focus

- **Long vowel teams *ai* and *ay***

See **Master Skills Tracker:** Teacher's Guide, page 548

Skills Tracker

Preteach | Teach/Practice/Apply | Review/Reinforce | Assess

Smart Words

Words are defined on pp. 4–5 of the student book. Page number of first appearance is listed below.

- **creature*, p. 8**
- **exist*, p. 8**
- **huge, p. 6**
- **locate*, p. 17**
- **squid, p. 12**
- **unusual*, p. 6**

*Spanish Cognates, **page 13**

Option 1: Decoding

 Conference

Ask students to read the Phonics Focus words on the inside back cover of *In Search of the Giant Squid*. If they struggle with decoding, proceed to individualized instruction.

 Individualized Instruction

For words with long vowel teams *ai* and *ay*: Have students use the Word Sort decoding routine on **page 21** to sort words by *ai* and *ay* spellings. Review that both spellings stand for the long *a* sound.

Option 2: Vocabulary

 Conference

Ask students to use some Smart Words listed on the inside back cover of *In Search of the Giant Squid* in an oral sentence. Review definitions on pages 4–5 as needed. If students demonstrate proficiency, proceed to individualized instruction.

 Individualized Instruction

Use the **Context Clues** vocabulary routine on **page 24** with the Smart Word *creature* as an example to help students use context clues to determine meaning.

Option 3: Fluency

 Conference

Ask students to read page 10 of *In Search of the Giant Squid* aloud. To work on expressive reading, proceed to individualized instruction.

 Individualized Instruction

Use page 10 of *In Search of the Giant Squid* and the **Read With Expression** fluency routine on **page 29** to have students practice expressive reading.

Comprehension

Use the questions below and the Wrap-Up on **page 77** to check comprehension and promote reader response.

After Chapter 1: *What happens when the sailors fire weapons at the Kraken? (It remains unharmed.)*

After Chapter 3: *In 2003, what makes a group of sailors think that the giant squid must be very dangerous? (A giant squid wraps its tentacle around their boat and shakes it.)*

End of Book: *Why is it so hard to study a live giant squid? (It is hard to find one. Even when one is captured, it can die trying to get away.)*

Resources	SAM Keywords
Wrap-Up, p. 77	Giant Squid
Reading Log, p. 105	Reading Log 44

Name _____

In Search of the Giant Squid

Build Understanding

▶ Scientists want to learn more about the giant squid. But there is a lot they already know. In each circle below, write one fact about the giant squid. An example is done for you.

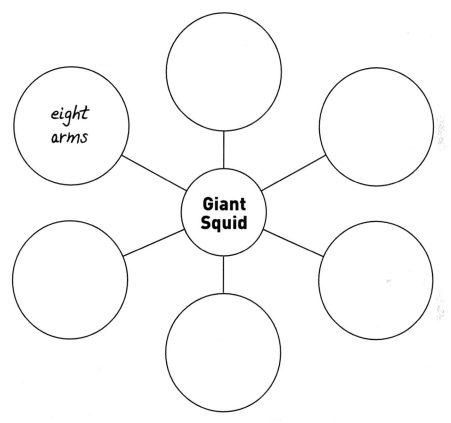

eight arms

Giant Squid

QuickWrite

▶ Why do you think that sailors called the giant squid a monster? Use facts from the circles above to explain your answer.

_____

_____

_____

Resource Links
Library Teaching Resources: p. 77
SAM Keyword: Giant Squid

Use with **Library Teaching Resources,** *page 76.*

BOOK 25 Conference Guide

Mookie Is Missing!
by **Carol Ghiglieri**

Genre	Pages	Lexile	Audio CD	Reading
Fiction	24	330	12 min 45 sec	Counts!

Summary

Someone has stolen Mookie the gorilla from the zoo. Willow, a zoo volunteer, is determined to find him. She partners with Joan, the ticket seller, to track down Mookie. They investigate strange noises, a stray banana peel, and other leads. But after noticing a scratch on Joan's arm, Willow soon figures out that Joan is the thief. The mystery is solved, and Mookie returns to the zoo.

Phonics Focus

- **Long _o_ vowel teams _oa_ and _ow_**

See **Master Skills Tracker:** Teacher's Guide, page 548

Skills Tracker

Preteach Teach/Practice/Apply Review/Reinforce Assess

Smart Words

Words are defined on pp. 4–5 of the student book. Page number of first appearance is listed below.

- **apartment*, p. 6**
- **director*, p. 8**
- **gorilla*, p. 11**
- **noise, p. 6**
- **occur*, p. 11**
- **zoo*, p. 6**

*Spanish Cognates, **page 13**

Option 1: **Decoding**

 Conference

Ask students to read the Phonics Focus words on the inside back cover of _Mookie Is Missing!_ If they struggle with decoding, proceed to individualized instruction.

 Individualized Instruction

For words with long _o_ vowel teams _oa_ and _ow_: Have students use the Word Sort decoding routine on **page 21** to sort words by _oa_ and _ow_ spellings. Review that both spellings can stand for the long _o_ sound.

Option 2: **Vocabulary**

 Conference

Ask students to use some Smart Words listed on the inside back cover of _Mookie Is Missing!_ in an oral sentence. Review definitions on pages 4–5 as needed. If students demonstrate proficiency, proceed to individualized instruction.

Individualized Instruction

Direct is the base of the Smart Word _director_ and the words _directed, directing, direction, directions, directly, directors,_ and _directs._ Use the **Extending Meaning** vocabulary routine on **page 22** to build student familiarity with morphological word families.

Option 3: **Fluency**

 Conference

Ask students to read page 6 of _Mookie Is Missing!_ aloud. To work on correct phrasing, proceed to individualized instruction.

 Individualized Instruction

Use pages 6–8 of _Mookie Is Missing!_ and the **Phrasing and Punctuation** fluency routine on **page 26** to have students practice correct phrasing.

Comprehension

Use the questions below and the Wrap-Up on **page 79** to check comprehension and promote reader response.

After Chapter 1: _What is the strange thing Willow notices when she looks out the window? Why does she think it's strange? (The zoo van is leaving late at night. Only Ms. Ramsey drives the van. Willow wonders why Ms. Ramsey is working so late.)_

After Chapter 3: _What clues make Willow think that Mookie might be in the apartment below hers? (the banana peel she slipped on in the lobby, and the banging noise)_

End of Book: _What are some things Joan lies about? (She says the scratch on her arm is from her cat and pretends not to know where Mookie is.)_

Resources	SAM Keywords
Wrap-Up, p. 79	Mookie
Reading Log, p. 105	Reading Log 44

Mookie Is Missing!

Build Understanding

▶ Read the list of events below. Then write the events in the order in which they happen in the book. The first one is done for you.

Events

Willow meets Dr. Sloan in his apartment.

Ms. Ramsey tells Willow that Joan doesn't own a cat.

Willow is awakened by strange noises.

Joan and Ms. Ramsey hear a noise from Joan's backyard.

Mr. Ramsey cries that someone stole Mookie.

First *Willow is awakened by strange noises.*

Second

Third

Next

Last

QuickWrite

▶ Do you think Willow is a good detective? Why or why not? Write at least two reasons.

_____

_____

_____

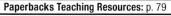

Resource Links

Paperbacks Teaching Resources: p. 79

SAM Keyword: Mookie

Use with **Library Teaching Resources,** page 78.

Samurai Fighters

by Mel Friedman

Genre	Pages	Lexile	Audio CD	Reading
Social Studies	24	300	15 min 46 sec	Counts!

Summary

The first Japanese samurai are warriors who serve and fight for the rich. Eventually, samurai gain independence. Their leader, the shogun, becomes more powerful than the emperor of Japan. Skilled samurai like the swordswoman Tomoe become legends. The shogun brings peace to Japan, but this creates less need for samurai. Unemployed samurai, called ronin, must find other work. Musashi is the last great samurai.

Phonics Focus

- **Long e vowel teams ea, ee, and ie**

See **Master Skills Tracker:** Teacher's Guide, page 548

Skills Tracker

Preteach   Teach/Practice/Apply   Review/Reinforce   Assess

Smart Words

Words are defined on pp. 4–5 of the student book. Page number of first appearance is listed below.

- clan*, p. 7
- defeat, p. 9
- emperor*, p. 8
- enemy*, p. 9
- legend*, p. 8
- samurai*, p. 7

*Spanish Cognates, **page 13**

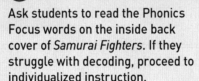

Option 1: Decoding

 Conference

Ask students to read the Phonics Focus words on the inside back cover of *Samurai Fighters*. If they struggle with decoding, proceed to individualized instruction.

 Individualized Instruction

For words with vowel teams ea, ee, and ie: Have students use the Word Sort decoding routine on **page 21** to sort words by *ee*, *ea*, and *ie* spellings. Review that all three spellings can stand for the long *e* sound.

Option 2: Vocabulary

Conference

Ask students to use some Smart Words listed on the inside back cover of *Samurai Fighters* in an oral sentence. Review definitions on pages 4–5 as needed. If students demonstrate proficiency, proceed to individualized instruction.

Individualized Instruction

Use the **Context Clues** vocabulary routine on **page 24** with the Smart Word *legend* as an example to help students use context clues to determine meaning.

Option 3: Fluency

 Conference

Ask students to read page 7 of *Samurai Fighters* aloud. To work on pacing, proceed to individualized instruction.

 Individualized Instruction

Use pages 7–9 of *Samurai Fighters* and the **Use Natural, Consistent Pace** fluency routine on **page 27** to have students practice correct pacing.

Comprehension

Use the questions below and the Wrap-Up on **page 81** to check comprehension and promote reader response.

After Chapter 1: *Why do Yoshiie's fighters respect him more than the emperor? (The emperor refuses to pay them, but Yoshiie rewards them.)*

After Chapter 3: *Who are the ronin, and what do they do to make money? (Ronin are former samurai who try to make money in other ways.)*

End of Book: *Why does Musashi become a legend? (He is never defeated in battle. His book about sword fighting is still read today.)*

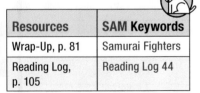

Resources	SAM Keywords
Wrap-Up, p. 81	Samurai Fighters
Reading Log, p. 105	Reading Log 44

Name _____

Samurai Fighters

Build Understanding

▶ Fill in the circles with details that tell about the samurai. You may describe their skills, behavior, clothing, and jobs. An example has been done for you.

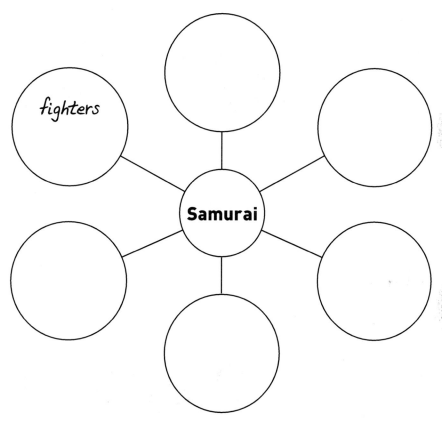

QuickWrite

▶ It's time to hire a new samurai. Write a job ad that describes the skills needed. Use at least two details from the book in your description.

_____

_____

_____

Resource Links
Library Teaching Resources: p. 81
SAM Keyword: Samurai Fighters

*Use with **Library Teaching Resources**, page 80.*

BOOK 27 Conference Guide

The Lost City

by **Mary Kay Carson**

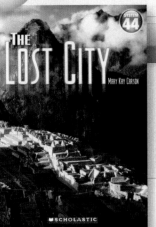

Genre	Pages	Lexile	Audio CD	Reading
Social Studies	**24**	**340**	**14 min 30 sec**	**Counts!**

Summary

In 1911, Hiram Bingham finds the ruins of Machu Picchu, an ancient city built by the Inca. The discovery helps experts learn about the Inca, an ancient people from Peru who ruled a huge empire in the 1400s. In 1572, Spain conquered the Inca. Although the empire is gone, remnants of the Inca civilization live on today.

Phonics Focus

- Prefixes *pre-* and *re-*
- Long *i, igh*
- Other long *i* spellings *ild, ind*
- Other long *o* spellings

See **Master Skills Tracker:** Teacher's Guide, page 548

Skills Tracker

Preteach   Teach/Practice/Apply   Review/Reinforce   Assess

Smart Words

Words are defined on pp. 4–5 of the student book. Page number of first appearance is listed below.

- ancient, p. 9
- empire*, p. 9
- reveal*, p. 9
- ruins*, p. 6
- site*, p. 13
- structure*, p. 13

*Spanish Cognates, **page 13**

Option 1: **Decoding**

 Conference

Ask students to read the Phonics Focus words on the inside back cover of *The Lost City*. If they struggle with decoding, proceed to individualized instruction.

Individualized Instruction

For words with prefixes *pre-* and *re*: Use the Word Parts routine on **page 18** to help students use prefixes.

For words with long *i* and *o* spellings: Have students use the Word Sort decoding routine on **page 21** to sort words by long *i* and long *o* sounds.

Option 2: **Vocabulary**

 Conference

Ask students to use some Smart Words listed on the inside back cover of *The Lost City* in an oral sentence. Review definitions on pages 4–5 as needed. If students demonstrate proficiency, proceed to individualized instruction.

 Individualized Instruction

The Smart Word *structure* can mean "something that has been built" or "the way something is put together." Use the **Multiple-Meaning Words** vocabulary routine on **page 23** with *structure* as an example to help students determine the correct meaning.

Option 3: **Fluency**

 Conference

Ask students to read page 10 of *The Lost City* aloud. To work on correct phrasing, proceed to individualized instruction.

 Individualized Instruction

Use pages 10–11 of *The Lost City* and the **Phrasing and Punctuation** fluency routine on **page 26** to have students practice correct phrasing.

Comprehension

Use the questions below and the Wrap-Up on **page 83** to check comprehension and promote reader response.

After Chapter 1: *What is Machu Picchu? (It is a mountain in Peru. It is also the city that the Inca built there.)*

After Chapter 3: *What are some of the mysteries of Machu Picchu? (Why was it built on top of a mountain? How did the Inca get heavy blocks up the mountain? Who lived there?)*

End of Book: *Why does the Inca empire disappear? (Spain attacks and conquers the empire.)*

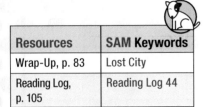

Resources	SAM Keywords
Wrap-Up, p. 83	Lost City
Reading Log, p. 105	Reading Log 44

Name _____

The Lost City

Build Understanding

▶ Details are bits of information. Write two details that tell about
each topic below. The first one is done for you.

Topic	Details
1. The Inca Empire *(Chapter 2)*	• By the late 1400s it was the largest nation on Earth. • Roads helped the Inca to control the empire.
2. Machu Picchu *(Chapter 3)*	
3. Explorers From Spain *(Chapter 4)*	
4. The Inca Today *(Chapter 5)*	

QuickWrite

▶ Why might the Inca have built Machu Picchu on a mountaintop?
Explain your answer using details from the book.

_____

_____

_____

Resource Links
Library Teaching Resources: p. 83
SAM Keyword: Lost City

Use with **Library Teaching Resources,** *page 82.*

Narrative of the Life of Frederick Douglass

Based on the Autobiography by Frederick Douglass

by **Terry West**

Narrative of the Life of **Frederick Douglass**

Terry West
A Graphic Classic Based on the Autobiography by Frederick Douglass
SCHOLASTIC

Genre	Pages	Lexile	Audio CD	Reading
Graphic Classic	**24**	**260**	**14 min 50 sec**	**Counts!**

Summary

This graphic classic based on Frederick Douglass's autobiography tells of his life as a slave and the terrible injustices he suffered. After one of his masters begins to teach him to read, Douglass yearns for freedom. He escapes and flees to the North. As a free man, Douglass speaks out against slavery and works to abolish it.

Phonics Focus

- **Multiple affixes**
- **Ending *-ed* with base change**
- **Review of suffix *-ly***

See **Master Skills Tracker:** Teacher's Guide, page 548

Skills Tracker
Preteach Teach/Practice/Apply Review/Reinforce Assess

Smart Words

Words are defined on pp. 4–5 of the student book. Page number of first appearance is listed below.

- cruel*, p. 13
- force, p. 7
- freedom, p. 10
- illegal*, p. 10
- refuse, p. 9
- slavery, p. 3

*Spanish Cognates, **page 13**

Option 1: **Decoding**

 Conference

Ask students to read the Phonics Focus words on the inside back cover of *Narrative of the Life of Frederick Douglass*. If they struggle with decoding, proceed to individualized instruction.

Individualized Instruction

For words with multiple affixes, *-ed* with base change, and suffix *-ly*: Use the Word Parts decoding routine on **page 18** to help students identify and use prefixes, suffixes, and inflectional endings.

Option 2: **Vocabulary**

 Conference

Ask students to use some Smart Words listed on the inside back cover of *Narrative of the Life of Frederick Douglass* in an oral sentence. Review definitions on pages 4–5 as needed. If students demonstrate proficiency, proceed to individualized instruction.

 Individualized Instruction

The idiom *her heart turned to stone* on the first panel of page 11 means "she became cruel and unfeeling." Build understanding of idioms using the **Idioms** vocabulary routine on **page 25** with this expression as an example.

Option 3: **Fluency**

 Conference

Ask students to read page 13 of *Narrative of the Life of Frederick Douglass* aloud. To work on expressive reading, proceed to individualized instruction.

 Individualized Instruction

Use page 13 of *Narrative of the Life of Frederick Douglass* and the **Read With Expression** fluency routine on **page 29** to have students practice expressive reading.

Comprehension

Use the questions below and the Wrap-Up on **page 85** to check comprehension and promote reader response.

After Page 9: *What are some of the terrible things the slave masters do to Frederick?* (They take him from his mother as a baby. They whip him, don't feed him enough, and make him sleep on the cold floor.)

After Page 15: *What important skill does Frederick learn that makes his heart yearn for freedom?* (He learns to read.)

End of Book: *What does Frederick do as a free man?* (He speaks at antislavery meetings and works to end slavery.)

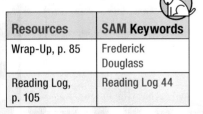

Resources	SAM Keywords
Wrap-Up, p. 85	Frederick Douglass
Reading Log, p. 105	Reading Log 44

Name _____

Narrative of the Life of Frederick Douglass

Build Understanding

▶ Write a thought that Frederick Douglass might have about each topic below. The first one is done for you.

I was taken away from her when I was a baby. I barely knew her.

1. His own mother

2. Slavery

3. Mrs. Auld

4. Reading

5. Mr. Covey

6. *The Liberator*
(the antislavery newspaper)

QuickWrite

▶ Slaves were not allowed to learn to read. But Frederick wanted to learn. Why was it so important to him? Write at least two sentences.

_____

_____

_____

Resource Links
Library Teaching Resources: p. 85
SAM Keyword: Frederick Douglass

Use with **Library Teaching Resources,** *page 84.*

Killer Croc
by Elizabeth Carney

Genre	Pages	Lexile	Audio CD	Reading
Science	24	430	18 min 5 sec	Counts!

Summary

In Burundi, Africa, a giant, killer crocodile prowls the shores of the Rusizi River and terrorizes villagers. A man named Patrice Faye names the croc Gustave and spends years trying to capture it. At one point, it seems that Gustave has died. Then in 2006, a giant croc kills ten people near Lake Tuanganyika, and the hunt for Gustave resumes.

Phonics Focus

- *r*-controlled vowels *ar*, *er*, *ir*, and *ur*
- Suffixes –*er* and –*or*

See **Master Skills Tracker:** Teacher's Guide, page 548

Skills Tracker

Preteach | Teach/Practice/Apply | Review/Reinforce | Assess

Smart Words

Words are defined on pp. 4–5 of the student book. Page number of first appearance is listed below.

- **capture***, p 15
- **dangerous**, p 8
- **expose***, p
- **fail**, p 16
- **reptile***, p 6
- **risk**, p 12
- **terror***, p 12

Spanish Cognates, **page 14*

Option 1: Decoding

 Conference

Ask students to read the Phonics Focus words on the inside back cover of *Killer Croc*. If they struggle with decoding, proceed to individualized instruction.

 Individualized Instruction

For words with *r*-controlled vowels *ar*, *er*, *ir*, and *ur*: Have students use the Word Sort decoding routine on **page 21** to sort words by *ar*, *er*, *ir*, and *ur* spellings.

For words with suffixes -*er* and -*or*: Use the Word Parts routine on **page 18** to help students identify and use suffixes.

Option 2: Vocabulary

 Conference

Ask students to use some Smart Words from the book in an oral sentence. Review definitions on pages 4–5 as needed. If students demonstrate proficiency, proceed to individualized instruction.

 Individualized Instruction

The Smart Word *dangerous* has many possible synonyms and antonyms. Use the **Extending Meaning** vocabulary routine on **page 22** to extend meaning.

Option 3: Fluency

 Conference

Ask students to read page 8 of *Killer Croc* aloud. To work on pacing, proceed to individualized instruction.

 Individualized Instruction

Use page 8 of *Killer Croc* and the **Read With Expression** fluency routine on **page 29** to have students practice expressive reading.

Comprehension

Use the questions below and the Wrap-Up on **page 87** to check comprehension and promote reader response.

After Chapter 1: *Why is Gustave so dangerous? (He's huge and kills large animals and people.)*

After Chapter 3: *Why doesn't Faye kill Gustave when he finds him? (He knows that such large crocs are rare. Capturing the croc alive will allow experts to study it.)*

End of Book: *What makes Faye think that Gustave might be dead? (Gustave disappears for a long time.)*

Resources	SAM **Keywords**
Wrap-Up, p. 87	Killer Croc
Reading Log, p. 105	Reading Log 44

Name _____

Killer Croc

Build Understanding

▶ Fill in the circles with words that tell about Gustave, the killer crocodile. An example is done for you.

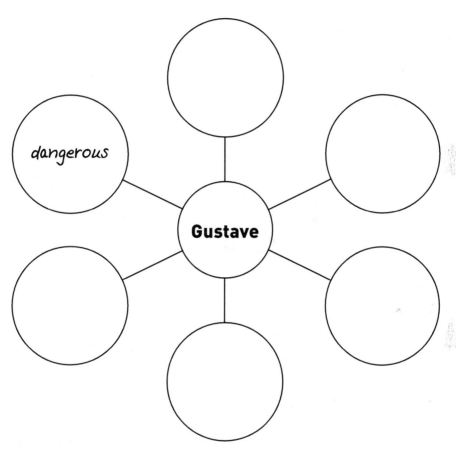

QuickWrite

▶ Why has no one been able to capture Gustave? Write a sentence that tells your opinion. Use at least one word from the circles above to support your answer.

_____

_____

_____

Dance Fever
by Brian Seibert

Genre	Pages	Lexile	Audio CD	Reading
Social Studies	24	420	16 min 46 sec	Counts

Summary

The dancers in this book have changed lives—their own and others'. In the 1920s, George Snowdon becomes famous for inventing swing dancing. In the 1950s Pedro Aguilar popularizes mambo. In the 1980s Tommy Johnson invents clowning and uses it as a way to keep kids out of gangs. Today, dancers are still creating new styles.

Phonics Focus

- r- controlled vowels *or*, *ore*
- /sh/ spellings *ci* and *ti*

See **Master Skills Tracker:** Teacher's Guide, page 548

Skills Tracker

Preteach Teach/Practice/Apply Review/Reinforce Assess

Smart Words

Words are defined on pp. 4–5 of the student book. Page number of first appearance is listed below.

- compete*, p. 8
- destination*, p. 8
- inspire*, p. 11
- partner, p. 9
- perform, p. 11
- rhythm*, p. 14
- tradition*, p. 6

*Spanish Cognates, **page 14**

Option 1: Decoding

 Conference

Ask students to read the Phonics Focus words on the inside back cover of *Dance Fever*. If they struggle with decoding, proceed to individualized instruction.

 Individualized Instruction

For words with *r*-controlled vowels *or* and *ore*: Have students use the Word Sort decoding routine on **page 21** to sort words according to their vowel spellings.

For words with /sh/ spellings *ci* and *ti*: Have students use the Word Sort routine to sort words by *ci* and *ti* spellings. Point out that both stand for the /sh/ sound.

Option 2: Vocabulary

 Conference

Ask students to use some Smart Words from the book in an oral sentence. Review definitions on pages 4–5 as needed. If students demonstrate proficiency, proceed to individualized instruction.

 Individualized Instruction

The Smart Word *tradition* means "a way of doing things that's handed down from one generation to the next." Use the **Context Clues** vocabulary routine on **page 24** with *tradition* as an example to help students use context clues to determine meaning.

Option 3: Fluency

 Conference

Ask students to read page 9 of *Dance Fever* aloud. To work on pacing, proceed to individualized instruction.

 Individualized Instruction

Use pages 9–12 of *Dance Fever* and the **Use Natural, Consistent Pace** fluency routine on **page 27** to have students practice reading at a natural pace.

Comprehension

Use the questions below and the Wrap-Up on **page 89** to check comprehension and promote reader response.

After Chapter 1: *Why is George Snowdon nicknamed "Shorty"?* (because he is only five feet tall)

After Chapter 2: *How does dance change Pete's life?* (Dance helps Pete pull away from the bad things that happened to him as a kid and become successful and famous.)

End of Book: *What rules does Tommy make kids in clowning performing groups follow?* (Kids have to go to school and get good grades. They can't be in a gang or use drugs.)

Resources	SAM Keywords
Wrap-Up, p. 89	Dance Fever
Reading Log, p. 105	Reading Log 44

Name _____

Dance Fever

Build Understanding

▶ How might the dancers in the book answer the questions below?
Write their responses in the speech bubbles. The first one is done for you.

I found ideas everywhere. I got them from watching people walk, listening to music, and from other dancers.

Question to Shorty:
Where did you get your ideas
for swing dancing?

Question to Pete:
How has dancing helped you?

Question to Eddie Torres:
What made you want to
learn how to dance?

Question to Tommy:
How has clowning helped others?

QuickWrite

▶ Can dancing change people's lives? Write a sentence that tells
your opinion. Use details from the book to support your answer.

_____

_____

_____

Resource Links
Library Teaching Resources: p. 89
SAM Keyword: Dance Fever

*Use with **Library Teaching Resources,** page 88.*

Weird Science Jobs
by **John DiConsiglio**

Genre	Pages	Lexile	Audio CD	Reading
Jobs	**24**	**430**	**18 min 5 sec**	**Counts!**

Summary

This book explores five weird science jobs. Florence Dunkel loves to eat and study bugs. James E. Starrs solves murder mysteries using science. Paul Doherty examines the science of baseball. Adriana Ocampo has a theory about why dinosaurs died out. Lastly, Carol Hirozawa Reiss maps the ocean floor.

Phonics Focus

- *r*-controlled vowels -*are*, -*air*, and -*ear*
- Suffixes -*er* and -*est*

See **Master Skills Tracker:**
Teacher's Guide, page 548

Skills Tracker

Preteach   Teach/Practice/Apply   Review/Reinforce   Assess

Smart Words

Words are defined on pp. 4–5 of the student book. Page number of first appearance is listed below.

- **investigate*, p. 7**
- **reason*, p. 7**
- **scientist*, p. 6**
- **search, p. 13**
- **solve*, p. 10**
- **study*, p. 6**
- **theory*, p. 17**

*Spanish Cognates, **page 14**

Option 1: **Decoding**

 Conference

Ask students to read the Phonics Focus words on the inside back cover of *Weird Science Jobs*. If they struggle with decoding, proceed to individualized instruction.

 Individualized Instruction

For words with *r*-controlled vowels -*air*, -*are*, and -*ear*: Have students use the Word Sort routine on **page 21** to sort words by -*are*, -*air*, and -*ear* spellings.

For words with suffixes -*er* and -*est*: Use the Word Parts decoding routine on **page 18** to help students identify and use suffixes.

Option 2: **Vocabulary**

 Conference

Ask students to use some Smart Words from the book in an oral sentence. Review definitions on pages 4–5 as needed. If students demonstrate proficiency, proceed to individualized instruction.

 Individualized Instruction

Science is the base of the Smart Word *scientist* and the words *scientists, sciences, scientific,* and *scientifically*. Use the **Extending Meaning** vocabulary routine on **page 22** to build student familiarity with morphological word families.

Option 3: **Fluency**

 Conference

Ask students to read page 14 of *Weird Science Jobs* aloud. To work on correct phrasing, proceed to individualized instruction.

 Individualized Instruction

Use page 14 of *Weird Science Jobs* and the **Phrasing and Punctuation** fluency routine on **page 26** to have students practice correct phrasing.

Comprehension

Use the questions below and the Wrap-Up on **page 91** to check comprehension and promote reader response.

After Chapter 1: *Why does Florence Dunkel believe people should eat bugs? (They are tasty, nutritious, and plentiful.)*

After Chapter 4: *What is Adriana Ocampo's theory about why the dinosaurs died? (An asteroid caused clouds of dirt to block out the sun. Earth became too cold to support life.)*

End of Book: *Why is Carol Hirozawa Reiss making a map of the ocean floor? (to find out how fast the ocean floor is spreading)*

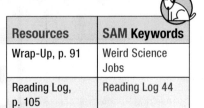

Resources	SAM Keywords
Wrap-Up, p. 91	Weird Science Jobs
Reading Log, p. 105	Reading Log 44

Name _____

Weird Science Jobs

Build Understanding

▶ As you read, identify the most important ideas in each chapter. Write a short summary of each chapter below. One has been done for you.

Chapter 1: "The Bug Eater"

_____

_____

Chapter 2: "Detective for the Dead"

Starrs uses scientific evidence to solve unsolved mysteries about dead

people. He solves the mystery of where Jesse James is buried.

Chapter 3: "Sports Science"

_____

_____

Chapter 4: "Dinosaur Disaster"

_____

_____

Chapter 5: "In the Deep"

_____

_____

QuickWrite

▶ Which science job in this book is the weirdest? Give at least one reason for your opinion.

_____

_____

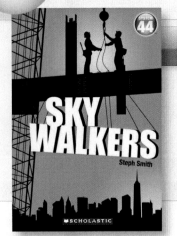

Sky Walkers
by Steph Smith

Genre	Pages	Lexile	Audio CD	Reading
Social Studies	24	440	17 min 10 sec	Counts!

Summary

Mohawk Indians have been ironworkers for over a century. Ironworkers build structures like bridges and skyscrapers. The job is sometimes deadly. Kyle Beauvais, a Mohawk ironworker, can't wear a safety rope while working. The hardest challenge Kyle has ever faced is clearing the rubble of the World Trade Center. Mohawks are proud of their ironworking tradition, but many are exploring less dangerous professions.

Phonics Focus

- **Diphthongs *oi* and *oy***
- ***ou* and *ow***
- **Suffixes *-ful* and *-less***

See **Master Skills Tracker:** Teacher's Guide, page 548

Skills Tracker
Preteach Teach/Practice/Apply Review/Reinforce Assess

Smart Words

Words are defined on pp. 4–5 of the student book. Page number of first appearance is listed below.

- balance*, p. 6
- community*, p. 8
- construct*, p. 8
- project*, p. 10
- rubble, p. 21
- success, p. 10
- vertical*, p. 16

*Spanish Cognates, **page 14**

Option 1: **Decoding**

 Conference

Ask students to read the Phonics Focus words on the inside back cover of *Sky Walkers*. If they struggle with decoding, proceed to individualized instruction.

 Individualized Instruction

For words with diphthongs *oi* and *oy*, and *ou* and *ow*: Have students use the Word Sort decoding routine on **page 21** to sort words by *oi*, *oy*, *ou*, and *ow* spellings.

For words with suffixes *-ful* and *-less*: Use the Word Parts decoding routine on **page 18** to help students use suffixes.

Option 2: **Vocabulary**

 Conference

Ask students to use some Smart Words from the book in an oral sentence. Review definitions on pages 4–5 as needed. If students demonstrate proficiency, proceed to individualized instruction.

 Individualized Instruction

The idiom *the worker froze* used in the first full paragraph of page 9 means "he couldn't move." Build understanding of idioms using the **Idioms** vocabulary routine on **page 25** with this expression as an example.

Option 3: **Fluency**

 Conference

Ask students to read page 17 of *Sky Walkers* aloud. To work on pacing, proceed to individualized instruction.

 Individualized Instruction

Use pages 17–19 of *Sky Walkers* and the **Use Natural, Consistent Pace** fluency routine on **page 27** to have students practice reading at a natural pace.

Comprehension

Use the questions below and the Wrap-Up on **page 93** to check comprehension and promote reader response.

After Chapter 1: *Why is it dangerous to be an ironworker? (Ironworkers work high above the ground. If they lose their balance, they will fall and die.)*

After Chapter 3: *What happens in 1907 to Mohawk men working on a bridge in Quebec City? (The bridge collapses and thirty-three Mohawk men die.)*

End of Book: *Why is Kyle's job so dangerous? (Kyle climbs to the top of vertical beams carrying heavy tools. He often doesn't wear ropes or have a safety net.)*

Resources	SAM Keywords
Wrap-Up, p. 93	Sky Walkers
Reading Log, p. 105	Reading Log 44

Name _____

Sky Walkers

Build Understanding

▶ What are the dangers of doing ironwork? Fill in the circles with examples. One is done for you.

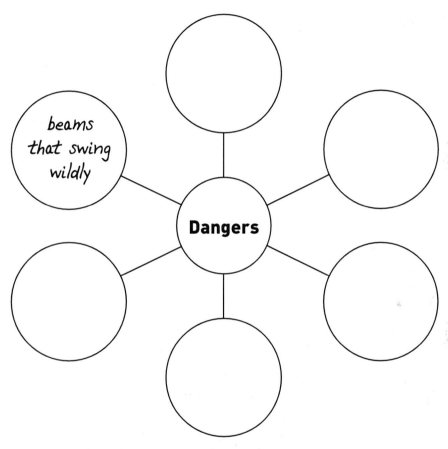

QuickWrite

▶ Would you like to be an ironworker? Why or why not? Explain your answer using details from the book.

_____

_____

_____

Resource Links
Library Teaching Resources: p. 93
SAM Keyword: Sky Walkers

Use with **Library Teaching Resources,** *page 92.*

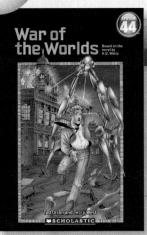

BOOK 33 · Conference Guide

War of the Worlds
Based on the Novel by H.G. Wells
by **Tod Olson** and **Terry West**

Genre	Pages	Lexile	Audio CD	Reading
Graphic Classic	**32**	**260**	**13 min 52 sec**	**Counts!**

Summary

In this classic retelling, the narrator warns people that Martians have landed, but no one believes him. When his wife goes missing, he searches for her and finds chaos and danger everywhere. He hides in an empty house. When he emerges from hiding, the Martians are dead. Martians could kill, but they couldn't protect themselves against the flu. The narrator reunites with his wife.

Phonics Focus

- *oo* and *ew*
- Prefixes *mid-*, *pre-*, and *sub-*
- Roots *dict* and *port*

See **Master Skills Tracker:** Teacher's Guide, page 548

Skills Tracker

Preteach | Teach/Practice/Apply | Review/Reinforce | Assess

Smart Words

Words are defined on pp. 4–5 of the student book. Page number of first appearance is listed below.

- crater*, p. 10
- disturbing, p. 8
- explode*, p. 15
- Martian*, p. 15
- meteor*, p. 8
- planet*, p. 7
- universe*, p. 7

*Spanish Cognates, **page 15**

Option 1: **Decoding**

 Conference

Ask students to read the Phonics Focus words on the inside back cover of *War of the Worlds*. If they struggle with decoding, proceed to individualized instruction.

Individualized Instruction

For words with *oo* and *ew*: Have students use the Word Sort decoding routine on **page 21** to sort by *oo* and *ew* spellings. Review that both can stand for the long *o* sound.

For words with prefixes *mid-* and *sub-*, and roots *dict* and *port*: Use the Word Parts routine on **page 18** to help students identify and use prefixes and roots.

Option 2: **Vocabulary**

 Conference

Ask students to use some Smart Words from the book in an oral sentence. Review definitions on page 4–5 as needed. If students demonstrate proficiency, proceed to individualized instruction.

 Individualized Instruction

A meteor is a fiery streak in the sky caused by a meteorite. Use the **Context Clues** vocabulary routine on **page 24** with the Smart Word *meteor* as an example to help students use context clues to determine meaning.

Option 3: **Fluency**

 Conference

Ask students to read page 10 of *War of the Worlds* aloud. To work on expressive reading, proceed to individualized instruction.

 Individualized Instruction

Use pages 10–11 of *War of the Worlds* and the **Read With Expression** fluency routine on **page 29** to have students practice expressive reading.

Comprehension

Use the questions below and the Wrap-Up on **page 95** to check comprehension and promote reader response.

After Page 11: *What happens to Ogilvy? (A Martian grabs him.)*

After Page 21: *What terrible things does the narrator witness? (Martians capturing people, the town being destroyed, people acting selfishly, and huge explosions)*

End of Book: *How does the Martian attack finally end? (The Martians die from the flu.)*

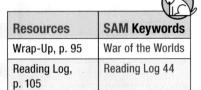

Resources	SAM Keywords
Wrap-Up, p. 95	War of the Worlds
Reading Log, p. 105	Reading Log 44

Name _____

War of the Worlds

Build Understanding

▶ Read the list of events below. Then write the events in the order in which they happen in the book. The first one is done for you.

Events

The narrator runs to warn people about the Martians.

The narrator and another man are trapped in an empty house.

The narrator realizes why the Martians have attacked Earth.

The Martians get the flu.

Ogilvy and the narrator examine a crater.

The narrator goes home and finds that his wife is missing.

First
Ogilvy and the narrator examine a crater.

Second

Third

Fourth

Next

Last

QuickWrite

▶ The narrator of this story has to be brave. Tell two things he does that show his bravery. Use details from the book to support your answer.

_____

_____

_____

Resource Links
Library Teaching Resources: p. 95
SAM Keyword: War of the Worlds

Use with **Library Teaching Resources,** page 94.

Everyday Heroes
by Patricia Kean

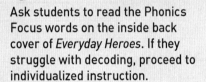

Genre	Pages	Lexile	Audio CD	Reading
Social Studies	32	440	24 min 48	Counts

Summary

Read about ordinary people who have risked their lives to help others. Four boys save a girl from an attack. Jose LeGrand stops a runaway car with a little girl inside it. Kelli Groves saves a choking baby. Jeremy Hernandez helps evacuate a school bus stuck on a collapsing bridge. And Wesley Autrey keeps a man from being run over by a train.

Phonics Focus

- *oo* and *u*
- Prefixes *dis-* and *mis-*
- Roots *rupt*, *struct*, and *scrib/script*

See **Master Skills Tracker:** Teacher's Guide, page 548

Skills Tracker

Preteach   Teach/Practice/Apply   Review/Reinforce   Assess

Smart Words

Words are defined on pp. 4–5 of the student book. Page number of first appearance is listed below.

- **discovery, p. 10**
- **distract*, p. 10**
- **distress, p. 10**
- **hesitate, p. 12**
- **instruct*, p. 19**
- **maneuver*, p. 19**
- **station*, p. 29**

*Spanish Cognates, **page 15**

Option 1: **Decoding**

 Conference

Ask students to read the Phonics Focus words on the inside back cover of *Everyday Heroes*. If they struggle with decoding, proceed to individualized instruction.

 Individualized Instruction

For words *oo* and *u*: Have students use the Word Sort routine on **page 21** to sort words by *oo* and *u* spellings. Review that both spellings can stand for the same sound.

For words with prefixes *dis-* and *mis-*, and roots *rupt*, *struct*, and *scrib/script*: Use the Word Parts decoding routine on **page 18** to help students identify and use prefixes and roots.

Option 2: **Vocabulary**

 Conference

Ask students to use some Smart Words from the book in an oral sentence. Review definitions on pages 4–5 as needed. If students demonstrate proficiency, proceed to individualized instruction.

 Individualized Instruction

Discover is the base of the Smart Word *discovery* and the words *discovered*, *discoveries*, *discovering*, and *discovers*. Use the **Extending Meaning** vocabulary routine on **page 22** to build familiarity with morphological word families.

Option 3: **Fluency**

Conference

Ask students to read page 13 of *Everyday Heroes* aloud. To work on pacing, proceed to individualized instruction.

Individualized Instruction

Use pages 13–15 of *Everyday Heroes* and the **Use Natural, Consistent Pace** fluency routine on **page 27** to have students practice correct pacing.

Comprehension

Use the questions below and the Wrap-Up on **page 97** to check comprehension and promote reader response.

After Chapter 1: *What happens to Samantha while she is riding her bike? (A car hits her, knocking her onto the grass. When she tries to get up, the driver pulls her back down.)*

After Chapter 3: *How do Jose and Maria help save Reiko? (They let Reiko's car smash into theirs, so that her car will come to a stop.)*

End of Book: *What does Wesley do to save Cameron? (Wesley lies on top of Cameron on the train tracks to protect Cameron from being run over.)*

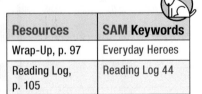

Resources	SAM Keywords
Wrap-Up, p. 97	Everyday Heroes
Reading Log, p. 105	Reading Log 44

Name _____

Everyday Heroes

Build Understanding

▶ Identify the most important things that happen in the chapters listed below. Then summarize each chapter in your own words. One has been done for you.

Chapter 1: "The Fantastic Four"

_____

_____

_____

Chapter 3: "A Baby's Life"

_____

_____

_____

Chapter 5: "Subway Superhero"

A man has a seizure and falls onto the train tracks. Wesley jumps off the

platform to save him. A train passes over them but they are unharmed.

Wesley is honored for being a hero.

QuickWrite

▶ Which story about everyday heroes inspires you the most? Explain your answer using details from the book.

_____

_____

_____

Fun Body Facts
by **Mary Kay Carson**

Genre	Pages	Lexile	Audio CD	Reading
Science	**32**	**430**	**26 min 26 sec**	**Counts**

Summary

This book is filled with fun facts about the human body. Readers learn scientific explanations for bodily functions such as vomit, runny noses, spit, earwax, scabs, and pus. The book also describes how these vital functions keep the body healthy.

Phonics Focus

- **a, au, and aw**
- **Suffixes -sion and -tion**
- **Roots auto, bio, and graph**

See **Master Skills Tracker:**
Teacher's Guide, page 548

Skills Tracker

Preteach Teach/Practice/Apply Review/Reinforce Assess

Smart Words

Words are defined on pp. 4–5 of the student book. Page number of first appearance is listed below.

- **bacteria*, p. 14**
- **cell*, p. 34**
- **digest*, p. 16**
- **healthy, p. 10**
- **normal*, p. 8**
- **produce*, p. 10**
- **react*, p. 24**

*Spanish Cognates, **page 15**

Option 1: **Decoding**

 Conference

Ask students to read the Phonics Focus words on the inside back cover of *Fun Body Facts*. If they struggle with decoding, proceed to individualized instruction.

Individualized Instruction

For words with a, au, and aw: Have students use the Word Sort decoding routine on **page 21** to sort words by a, au, and aw spellings.

For words with suffixes –sion and –tion, and roots auto, bio, and graph: Use the Word Parts routine on **page 18** to help students identify and use suffixes and roots.

Option 2: **Vocabulary**

 Conference

Ask students to use some Smart Words from the book in an oral sentence. Review definitions on pages 4–5 as needed. If students demonstrate proficiency, proceed to individualized instruction.

 Individualized Instruction

The Smart Word *bacteria* is defined in the book as "very tiny creatures that live on and inside you." Use the **Context Clues** vocabulary routine on **page 24** with *bacteria* as an example to help students use context clues to determine meaning.

Option 3: **Fluency**

 Conference

Ask students to read page 6 of *Fun Body Facts* aloud. To work on correct phrasing, proceed to individualized instruction.

 Individualized Instruction

Use page 6 of *Fun Body Facts* and the **Phrasing and Punctuation** fluency routine on **page 26** to have students practice correct phrasing.

Comprehension

Use the questions below and the Wrap-Up on **page 99** to check comprehension and promote reader response.

After Chapter 1: *What causes a burp? (swallowed air that needs to get out)*

After Chapter 3: *What causes body odor and bad breath? (the bacteria that eat armpit sweat and mouth plaque)*

End of Book: *Why is it good to learn about these bodily functions? (to be aware that they help keep the body healthy)*

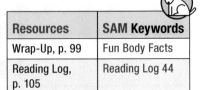

Resources	SAM Keywords
Wrap-Up, p. 99	Fun Body Facts
Reading Log, p. 105	Reading Log 44

Name _____

Fun Body Facts

Build Understanding

▶ Details are bits of information. Fill in the chart below with details that tell what each bodily function does to keep your body healthy. The first one is done for you.

Bodily Function	Details
Sweat (Pages 9–10)	*cools down your body*
Vomit (Pages 23–26)	
Snot (Pages 27–29)	
Spit (Pages 29–30)	
Earwax (Pages 30–31)	
Scabs (Pages 32–34)	

QuickWrite

▶ Would you be better off if your body didn't make snot? Tell why or why not. Use details from above to support your answer.

_____

_____

_____

Resource Links
Library Teaching Resources: p. 99
SAM Keyword: Fun Body Facts

Use with **Library Teaching Resources,** page 98.

BOOK 36 · Conference Guide

The Legend of Sleepy Hollow
Based on the Novel by Washington Irving

Adapted by **Adam Grant**

Genre	Pages	Lexile	Audio CD	Reading Counts!
Classic Retelling	34	320	26 min 18 sec	✓

Summary

In this classic retelling, Ichabod Crane, the skinny teacher, and handsome Brom both love Katrina. Riding home from Katrina's party, Ichabod encounters the Headless Horseman and vanishes. Brom, who may know something about the disappearance, marries Katrina. Ichabod becomes another part of the Headless Horseman's legend.

Phonics Focus

- Prefix *tri-*
- Suffixes *-able* and *-ible*
- Roots *scope*, *tele*, and *vis/vid*

See **Master Skills Tracker:** Teacher's Guide, page 548

Skills Tracker

Preteach Teach/Practice/Apply Review/Reinforce Assess

Smart Words

Words are defined on pp. 4–5 of the student book. Page number of first appearance is listed below.

- comfortable, p. 7
- coward*, p. 13
- haunted, p. 6
- impress*, p. 11
- panic*, p. 8
- terrible*, p. 26
- vanish, p. 27

*Spanish Cognates, **page 15**

Option 1: Decoding

 Conference

Ask students to read the Phonics Focus words on the inside back cover of *The Legend of Sleepy Hollow*. If they struggle with decoding, proceed to individualized instruction.

 Individualized Instruction

For words with prefix *tri-*, suffixes *-able* and *-ible*, and roots *scope*, *tele*, and *vis/vid*: Use the Word Parts decoding routine on **page 18** to help students identify and use prefixes, suffixes, and roots.

Option 2: Vocabulary

 Conference

Ask students to use some Smart Words from the book in an oral sentence. Review definitions on pages 4–5 as needed. If students demonstrate proficiency, proceed to individualized instruction.

 Individualized Instruction

Comfort is the base of the Smart Word *comfortable* and the words *comfortably*, *comforted*, *comforting*, and *discomfort*. Use the **Extending Meaning** routine on **page 22** to build student familiarity with morphological word families.

Option 3: Fluency

 Conference

Ask students to read page 28 of *The Legend of Sleepy Hollow* aloud. To work on expressive reading, proceed to individualized instruction.

 Individualized Instruction

Use pages 28–29 of *The Legend of Sleepy Hollow* and the **Read With Expression** fluency routine on **page 29** to have students practice expressive reading.

Comprehension

Use the questions below and the Wrap-Up on **page 101** to check comprehension and promote reader response.

After Chapter 1: *What is the scariest story that people tell in Sleepy Hollow? (the story of the Headless Horseman)*

After Chapter 4: *Ichabod and Brom want the same thing. What is it? (They both want to marry Katrina, the prettiest girl in town.)*

End of Book: *What happens to Ichabod on his way home from Katrina's party? (The Headless Horseman chases Ichabod and throws something at him. Ichabod vanishes.)*

Resources	SAM **Keywords**
Wrap-Up, p. 101	Sleepy Hollow
Reading Log, p. 105	Reading Log 44

Name _____

The Legend of Sleepy Hollow

Build Understanding

▶ Read the list of events below. Then write the events in the order in which they happen in the book. The first one is done for you.

Events

Ichabod goes to Katrina's party.

Ichabod's hat and a broken pumpkin are found next to the bridge.

Ichabod vanishes.

Ichabod falls in love with Katrina.

Brom warns Ichabod about the Headless Horseman.

Ichabod becomes the teacher of Sleepy Hollow.

First
Ichabod becomes the teacher of Sleepy Hollow.

Second

Third

Fourth

Next

Last

QuickWrite

▶ If Ichabod hadn't vanished, would Katrina have married him? Tell why or why not. Use details from the story to support your answer.

_____

_____

_____

Resource Links
Library Teaching Resources: p. 101
SAM Keyword: Sleepy Hollow

Use with **Library Teaching Resources**, *page 100.*

Name _____

Word Sort

▶ Use this page to sort words by sound or spelling. Write the sounds or spellings you will use in the top row of the chart below. Then, fill in each column with words that have that sound or spelling.

SOUND OR SPELLING _____	SOUND OR SPELLING _____	SOUND OR SPELLING _____	SOUND OR SPELLING _____

Resource Links
Library Teaching Resources: p. 102
SAM Keyword: Word Sort 44

Name _____

Vocabulary Builder

▶ Use the chart below to list new words you come across in your reading. For each word, write a definition and a short sentence that uses the word.

Book Title _____

NEW WORD	DEFINITION	MY SENTENCE

Resource Links
Library Teaching Resources: p. 103
SAM Keyword: Vocabulary Builder 44

Name _____

Fluency Checklist

▶ Use this checklist to keep a record of progress. Write the date and the reader's name. Then, make checkmarks to show what improved. Add helpful comments if you like.

Date _____

Name _____

Accuracy

___ Skipped words

___ Read every word

___ Self-corrected

Speed

___ Too slow

___ Just right

___ Too fast

Expression

___ Paid attention to end punctuation

___ Paused at commas and used phrasing

___ Read with expression

Resource Links
Library Teaching Resources: p. 104
SAM Keyword: Fluency Checklist 44

Name _____

Reading Log

▶ Use this page to record your daily reading.

DATE	TITLE	STARTING PAGE	ENDING PAGE	NOTES

Resource Links
Library Teaching Resources: p. 105
SAM Keyword: Reading Log 44

Answer Key

The following are answers from the Build Understanding portions of the Wrap-Ups.

Book 1: *Hunt and Kill: A Look at Predators*, p. 31
Answers may vary. Possible answers include:

They are top predators; They attack seals and big fish; They swim fast; They have big teeth; They can kill people.

Book 2: *Messy Jobs*, p. 33
Answers may vary. Possible answers include:

Ship Painter: The old paint and the new paint get all over me!
Podiatrist: Cutting people's nails and taking off bumps can be messy!
Motocross Racer: Mud flies onto my bike and my clothes!

Book 3: *Sports Bloopers*, p. 35
Answers may vary. Possible answers include:

She tries to jump over the hurdle. He runs into the net. The ball bounces over the wall. He is kicked in the head. She steps the wrong way.

Book 4: *Fast!*, p. 37
Answers may vary. Possible answers include:

They can run 71 miles per hour. Their claws grip the ground. They get hot when they run. They have to rest after running. They run faster than speed limits!

Book 5: *I Do Not Eat Worms (and Other Poems)*, p. 39
Answers may vary. Possible answers include:

2. My brother eats worms!
3. I want to sing on TV.
4. My Grandma is a good cook and we love each other a lot.
5. I don't always like to do homework, but I will finish it.

Book 6: *Wonders of the World*, p. 41
Answers may vary. Possible answers include:

Pyramids of Giza: The pyramids are made of stone blocks. They are really old. The kings of Egypt are buried inside the pyramids.
Great Wall of China: The Great Wall is so long that it can be seen from space. The wall was built to protect China.
Statue of Liberty: The Statue of Liberty was a gift from France. It was put up in 1886. It is in New York Harbor.

Book 7: *Mystery Photo*, p. 43
Answers may vary. Possible answers include:

Pizza: It has a crust. It is topped with sauce and cheese.
Soccer Ball: Watch the World Cup.
Lobster: They come in many colors. But every one turns red when cooked.
Skyscraper: You need steel, concrete, and glass to construct it.

Stop Sign: It has eight sides. Its shape is called an octagon.
Book: You are looking at one right now!
Polar Bear: It has two layers of white fur.

Book 8: *Travels With Mapman*, p. 45
Washington: They have a milk carton boat race.
Idaho: They have a tug of war over a pit of potatoes.
Utah: It is called the Great Salt Lake.
Arizona: The Colorado River runs through Arizona.
New York: Albany is the capital.

Book 9: *The Gift*, p. 47
Second: Kendra goes to the guitar store.
Next: Kendra sells her guitar.
Then: Kendra buys a watch chain.
Last: Chet and Kendra open their gifts.

Book 10: *Gross Bugs!*, p. 49
Answers may vary. Possible answers include:

Bed Bug: Bed bugs bite people. They live in beds.
Tick: Ticks live outdoors. They can get stuck in your skin.
Cockroach: There are more than 3,000 kinds of them. Most live inside.
Slug: Slugs are slimy. They don't have legs so they glide.
Maggot: Maggots eat skin. Doctors sometimes use them to help heal a cut.
Stink Bug: They give off a bad smell when they are scared. They have a beak.
Carpet Beetle: They can destroy carpets and clothes. Young carpet beetles are soft.

Book 11: *Signs*, p. 51
Stop Signs: Stop signs tell people to stop.
Caution Signs: Caution signs tell people to be careful. They warn that something shocking could happen.
Animal Signs: Animal signs warn people that animals are near.
No! Signs: No! signs tell that something is not allowed.

Book 12: *Fashion Flashback*, p. 53
Answers may vary. Possible answers include:

light and loose dresses, shoulder pads, preppy shirts, stretched-out shirts, jeans with holes

Book 13: *Button Your Lip and Other Idioms*, p. 55
2. Do not talk
3. Do not tell a secret
4. To be right
5. Slow down
6. Think about a problem

7. Saying the wrong thing at the wrong time
8. Hurry

Book 14: *African Journey*, p. 57
Answers may vary. Possible answers include:

Going on Safari: It is very dry here. Many animals migrate in the Serengeti National Park.
Animal Buddies: Zebras help each other watch for dangerous lions. Birds help keep elephants' skin clean by eating bugs.
On the Hunt: Cheetahs can run up to 70 miles per hour. A group of lions is called a pride.
Visiting the Maasai: The Maasai raise cattle for milk and meat. The Maasai build their houses in a circle.

Book 15: *Ripped From the Headlines*, p. 59
Answers may vary. Possible answers include:

"Stranger Danger!": Palmira Gonzalez-Jiminez is in gym class when a man grabs her. Her friends rescue her from the man.
"Falling Baby!": Felix Vasquez is outside a burning building. A mother and her baby are trapped inside. The mother tosses the baby to Felix. Felix safely catches the baby.
"Trapped!": Aron Ralston is hiking when a big rock rolls onto his arm and traps him. After five days he cuts off his arm and hikes to a hospital for help.

Book 16: *Win or Lose?*, p. 61
Answers may vary. Possible answers include:

Ray: Dan may make us lose the game.
Dan: I hope that I can play soccer.
Grace: Dan needs a chance to play.

Book 17: *Cool Jobs in Basketball*, p. 63
Answers may vary. Possible answers include:

Tony: I write about pro basketball for a Web site. I get to travel to basketball games and talk to athletes. I am living my dream!
Keith: I'm a trainer for professional basketball teams. I teach exercises to hurt athletes to help them get better.

Book 18: *Meet the Dragon Slayers*, p. 65
Answers may vary. Possible answers include:

1. Fire Chief Brown starts his own fire and rescue crew called the Dragon Slayers.
2. Fire Chief Brown gets teens to volunteer. The teens get the same training as police and firefighters.
4. The boy's friends call the Dragon Slayers for help. The Slayers rush to the scene of the accident.
5. The Slayers make sure the boy is breathing. They stop his bleeding. They stay up with him all night until a plane comes to take him to the hospital.

Book 19: *Crash!*, p. 67
Answers may vary. Possible answers include:

Chapter 1: An asteroid is a big rock found in space. If an asteroid hits Earth it will cause a lot of damage. Scientists follow the paths of asteroids so we know if one may hit Earth.

Chapter 3: Asteroids are left over from when planets formed billions of years ago. Experts study them to learn about what Earth was like back then. Telescopes help experts see more asteroids.

Book 20: *The Champ and Other Stories*, p. 69
Answers may vary. Possible answers include:

Kelly: The lesson I learned is to not count my chickens before they hatch.

Andy: The lesson I learned is to never cry wolf.

Book 21: *From the Heart*, p. 71
2. Adrian goes to a hospital in Arkansas. Doctors find a new heart for him, but his body may reject it.

3. Doctors begin Adrian's surgery as soon as the heart arrives.

4. The president of Mexico visits Adrian at the hospital. The surgery works! Adrian is still at risk, but has a good chance of recovery.

Book 22: *The Mummy King*, p. 73
Answers may vary. Possible answers include:

Chapter 1: They believe Tut will come back to life.

Chapter 2: Howard Carter's job is to study items from long ago. He discovers King Tut's tomb.

Chapter 3: He finds three coffins surrounded King Tut's mummy.

Book 23: *Disaster!*, p. 75
Answers may vary. Possible answers include:

Kaci: The tornado was really scary. It knocked down trees and damaged a lot of homes. I was scared for my family.

Fitri: We lost everything we owned in the tsunami. So many people lost loved ones also. I'm grateful that my family survived.

Troy: Hurricane Katrina was one of the worst things that I've been through. We lost many things in the hurricane. I'm glad to be back in New Orleans now, though.

Book 24: *In Search of the Giant Squid*, p. 77
Answers may vary. Possible answers include:
can be 60 feet long, huge eyes, two tentacles, suckers, beak, no bones

Book 25: *Mookie Is Missing!*, p. 79
Second: Ms. Ramsey cries that someone stole Mookie.

Third: Willow meets Dr. Sloan in his apartment.

Next: Ms. Ramsey tells Willow that Joan doesn't own a cat.

Last: Joan and Ms. Ramsey hear a noise from Joan's backyard.

Book 26: *Samurai Fighters*, p. 81
Answers may vary. Possible answers include:
two swords, body armor, masks, helmets, long robes, hair long in back

Book 27: *The Lost City*, p. 83
Answers may vary. Possible answers include:

Machu Picchu: It was built around 1400. It sits atop a mountain.

Explorers From Spain: They came to Peru in 1532. They wanted Spain to rule the Inca empire.

The Inca Today: Modern Inca still live in Peru. Many still speak Quechua and Aymara, the old Inca languages.

Book 28: *Narrative of the Life of Frederick Douglass*, p. 85
Answers may vary. Possible answers include:

2. I was often hungry and cold. Many slaves were whipped a lot.

3. She taught me to read. At first she was kind but soon she became mean.

4. The more I read, the more I hated being a slave.

5. He beat me often but I learned that I would always be free in spirit.

6. This paper made me feel happy. I wanted to help end slavery.

Book 29: *Killer Croc*, p. 87
Answers may vary. Possible answers include:
reptile, at least 20 feet long, weighs about 2,000 pounds, lives in Burundi, hasn't been caught

Book 30: *Dance Fever*, p. 89
Answers may vary. Possible answers include:

Pete: Dancing helped me get past my anger.

Eddie Torres: A girl I liked laughed at me because I couldn't dance. I didn't want that to happen again.

Tommy: Clowning has motivated kids to stay in school, get good grades, and stay out of gangs.

Book 31: *Weird Science Jobs*, p. 91
Answers may vary. Possible answers include:
Chapter 1: Florence Dunkel studies bugs and eats them! She says most people have probably eaten bugs without knowing it.

Chapter 3: Paul Doherty is a scientist who uses physics to study baseball. He says science can help people play better.

Chapter 4: Adriana Ocampo has a theory about what killed the dinosaurs. She thinks an asteroid hit Earth and made a giant dust cloud. This cloud blocked out the sun, so the dinosaurs froze.

Chapter 5: Carol Hirozawa Reiss uses a special submarine to map the ocean floor. She wants to find out if the ocean floor is spreading.

Book 32: *Sky Walkers*, p. 93
Answers may vary. Possible answers include:
fainting in the heat, falling due to wind, slipping in the rain, panicking on a beam, beams that collapse

Book 33: *War of the Worlds*, p. 95
Second: The narrator runs to warn people about the Martians.

Third: The narrator goes home and finds his wife is missing.

Fourth: The narrator and another man are trapped in an empty house.

Next: The narrator realizes why the Martians have attacked Earth.

Last: The Martians get the flu.

Book 34: *Everyday Heroes*, p. 97
Answers may vary. Possible answers include:

Chapter 1: A man tries to hurt a teenage girl, but boys from her town are able to help her.

Chapter 3: Kelli Groves is able to save a baby who is not breathing by remembering how to do the Heimlich maneuver she learned in school.

Book 35: *Fun Body Facts*, p. 99
Answers may vary. Possible answers include:

Vomit: gets rid of germs in your stomach

Snot: stops germs and dirt from getting into your lungs

Spit: helps you swallow and digest your food

Earwax: traps dirt, dust, and germs that float into your ears

Scabs: keep dirt and bacteria out of your cuts

Book 36: *The Legend of Sleepy Hollow*, p. 101
Second: Ichabod falls in love with Katrina.

Third: Ichabod goes to Katrina's party.

Fourth: Brom warns Ichabod about the Headless Horseman.

Next: Ichabod vanishes.

Last: Ichabod's hat and a broken pumpkin are found next to the bridge.

Index

SYSTEM 44

Genres

Graphic Organizers

Instructional Routines

Vocabulary-Building Strategies

Wrap-Ups

Book Cover Credits

HUNT AND KILL: A LOOK AT PREDATORS by Rob Camacho. Copyright © 2009 by Scholastic Inc. Published by Scholastic Inc. Cover: Peter Lilja/Getty Images.

MESSY JOBS by Alan Takamura. Copyright © 2009 by Scholastic Inc. Published by Scholastic Inc. Cover: Steve Giberson/Transworld.

SPORTS BLOOPERS by Peter Gutiérrez. Copyright © 2009 by Scholastic Inc. Published by Scholastic Inc. Cover: Lucy Nicholson/Reuters.

FAST! THE WORLD'S FASTEST COUCH AND OTHER FAST THINGS by Juliette Caggiano. Copyright © 2009 by Scholastic Inc. Published by Scholastic Inc. Cover: Raymonds Press Agency.

I DO NOT EAT WORMS AND OTHER POEMS by Tina Posner, illustrated by Fernanda Cohen. Cover illustration copyright © 2009 by Neil Webb. Published by Scholastic Inc.

WONDERS OF THE WORLD by Joshua Davis. Copyright © 2009 by Scholastic Inc. Published by Scholastic Inc. Cover: (bl) Brian A. Vikander/Mira.com/drr.net, (tl) Joseph Feltham/iStockphoto, (tr) David Sutherland/drr.net, (br) Wesley Hitt/Getty Images, (c) NASA.

MYSTERY PHOTO by Nancy Honovich. Copyright © 2009 by Scholastic Inc. Published by Scholastic Inc. Cover: (bl) photolibrary.com pty.ltd/Index Open, (cl) Donnelly Marks, (lc) Greg Vote/VStock/Index Open, (tl) Donnelly Marks, (ct) AbleStock/ Index Open, (rc) Photos.com Select/Index Open, (br) Keith Levit Photography/Index Open.

TRAVELS WITH MAPMAN by Susan O'Connor, illustrated by Jim McMahon. Copyright © 2009 by Scholastic Inc. Published by Scholastic Inc. Cover: Yvonne Silver.

THE GIFT based on the short story "The Gift of the Magi" by O. Henry, adapted by Michael Leviton, illustrated by Julia Denos. Copyright © 2009 by Scholastic Inc. Published by Scholastic Inc. Cover: (background) Lisa Thornberg/iStockphoto.

GROSS BUGS! by Kim Feltes. Copyright © 2009 by Scholastic Inc. Published by Scholastic Inc. Cover: Eye of Science/Photo Researchers, Inc., (bl) Doug Wechsler/Animals Animals, (tl) Maryann Frazier/Photo Researchers, Inc., (tc) Mark Smith/Photo Researchers, Inc., (br) Sinclair Stammers/Photo Researchers, Inc.

SIGNS by Susan O'Connor. Copyright © 2009 by Scholastic Inc. Published by Scholastic Inc.

FASHION FLASHBACK by Richard Camden. Copyright © 2009 by Scholastic Inc. Published by Scholastic Inc. Cover: (l) Reuters/Corbis, (c) Ron Stewart/SuperStock, (r) Hulton Archive/Getty Images.

BUTTON YOUR LIP AND OTHER IDIOMS by Polly Downes, illustrated by Debbie Palen. Illustrations copyright © 2009 by Debbie Palen. Published by Scholastic Inc.

AFRICAN JOURNEY by Leslie Bakke and Susan O'Connor. Copyright © 2009 by Scholastic Inc. Published by Scholastic Inc. Cover: Leslie Bakke, (background) Felix Möcke/iStockphoto.

RIPPED FROM THE HEADLINES by Peter Gutiérrez. Copyright © 2009 by Scholastic Inc. Published by Scholastic Inc. Cover: © Steve Robertson/Zuma Press, (background) Stephen Firmender.

WIN OR LOSE? by Sunita Apte, illustrated by Lawrence Christmas. Copyright © 2009 by Scholastic Inc. Published by Scholastic Inc.

COOL JOBS IN BASKETBALL by Peter Gutiérrez. Copyright © 2009 by NBA Properties, Inc. Published by Scholastic Inc. Cover: Adam Borkowski/Shutterstock.

MEET THE DRAGON SLAYERS by Julia Campbell. Copyright © 2009, 2004 by Scholastic Inc. Published by Scholastic Inc. Cover: Axel Koester/People Weekly.

CRASH! by Steph Smith. Copyright © 2009 by Scholastic Inc. Published by Scholastic Inc. Cover: Denis Scott/Corbis.

THE CHAMP AND OTHER STORIES adapted by Michael Leviton based on three fables by Aesop, illustrated by Lisa K. Weber. Illustrations copyright © 2009 by Lisa K. Weber. Published by Scholastic Inc.

FROM THE HEART by Meredith Phillips. Copyright © 2009 by Scholastic Inc. Published by Scholastic Inc. Cover: Kelley Cooper/Arkansas Children's Hospital, (background) Sebastian Kaulitzki/Shutterstock.

THE MUMMY KING by Sean McCollum. Cover illustration copyright © 2004 by Steve Chorney. Published by Scholastic Inc.

DISASTER! by Sean Price. Copyright © 2009 by Scholastic Inc. Published by Scholastic Inc. Cover: Dave Martin/AP Images.

IN SEARCH OF THE GIANT SQUID by Britt Norlander. Copyright © 2009 by Scholastic Inc. Published by Scholastic Inc. Cover: Flip Nicklin/Mindset Pictures, (inset) Onrequest Images, Inc./Jupiter Images.

MOOKIE IS MISSING! by Carol Ghiglieri, illustrated by Monika Melnychuck. Copyright © 2009, 2004 by Scholastic Inc. Published by Scholastic Inc.

SAMURAI FIGHTERS by Mel Friedman, illustrated by Red Hansen. Illustrations copyright © 2003 by Red Hansen. Published by Scholastic Inc.

THE LOST CITY by Mary Kay Carson. Copyright © 2009 by Scholastic Inc. Published by Scholastic Inc. Cover: Jim Erickson/Corbis.

NARRATIVE OF THE LIFE OF FREDERICK DOUGLASS adapted by Terry M. West, cover illustration by Michael Lilly. Copyright © 2009, 1999 by Scholastic Inc. Published by Scholastic Inc.

KILLER CROC by Elizabeth Carney. Copyright © 2009 by Scholastic Inc. Published by Scholastic Inc. Cover: Frans Lanting/Minden Pictures.

DANCE FEVER by Brian Seibert. Copyright © 2009 by Scholastic Inc. Published by Scholastic Inc. Cover: (bl) PM Images/Getty Images, (tc) Rubberball/Getty Images, (tr) Bruce Talbot/DK Stock/Getty Images, (br) Mike Powell/Getty Images.

WEIRD SCIENCE JOBS by John DiConsiglio. Copyright © 2009, 2003 by Scholastic Inc. Published by Scholastic Inc. Cover: White Packert/The Image Bank/Getty Images.

SKY WALKERS by Steph Smith. Copyright © 2009 by Scholastic Inc. Published by Scholastic Inc. Cover: PhotoLink/Getty Images.

WAR OF THE WORLDS based on the novel by H.G. Wells, by Tod Olson and Terry West, illustrated by Phil Xavier and Nimbus Studios. Copyright © 2009, 2002 by Scholastic Inc. Published by Scholastic Inc.

EVERYDAY HEROES by Patricia Kean. Copyright © 2009 by Scholastic Inc. Published by Scholastic Inc. Cover: (tl) Lori Adamski-Peek, (tr) Dynamic Graphics/Jupiter Images, (bl) Dan Henry/AP Images, (br) Ray Tammara/Getty Images.

FUN BODY FACTS by Mary Kay Carson, illustrated by Jeffrey Lindberg. Illustrations copyright © 2003 Jeffrey Lindberg. Published by Scholastic Inc.

THE LEGEND OF SLEEPY HOLLOW based on the Novel by Washington Irving, adapted by Adam Grant, cover illustration by Jim Nelson. Cover illustration copyright © 2003 by Jim Nelson. Published by Scholastic Inc.